Clarity in Religious Education

Clarity
in
Religious
Education

ROBERT YORKE O'BRIEN

Religious Education Press

Birmingham   Alabama

Library of Congress Cataloging in Publication Data

O'Brien, Robert Yorke.
   Clarity in religious education.

   Includes index.
   1.   Christian education.   I.   Title.
BV1471.2.025   268   78-3497
ISBN 0-89135-013-6

2 3 4 5 6 7 8 9 10

Religious Education Press, Inc.
1531 Wellington Rd.
Birmingham, Alabama 35209

*Religious Education Press publishes books and educational materials ex-
clusively in religious education and in areas closely related to religious
education. It is committed to enhancing and professionalizing religious education through the publication of significant scholarly and popular works.*

To
ANNIE, PATRICK, MEGAN, KATIE
from
whose lives
love has been learned

CONTENTS

INTRODUCTION

The thesis put forward by this book is: clarity will enrich religious education. In twelve chapters means to foster clarity are proposed. Certainly the pursuit of clarity is not the whole secret of attaining top-quality religious education programs. Administrative organization, finances, textbook selections, curricula and syllabi (scope and sequence), personnel recruitment and development are important factors. Moreover they are rather tangible, objective items, whereas clarity seems an ethereal and highly subjective criterion. So when religious education programs are languishing the usual reaction is to change the structure: to centralize, or if centralization was the most recent change then decentralization is proposed. The commercial interests have made the not-so-subtle suggestion that quality can be bought for a price. But often the dissatisfaction concerns expensive materials purchased with the presumption that they were part of the solution rather than part of the problem. Textbooks are tools. Skilled workers get good results with adequate tools; poor artisans get poor results using the best tools. The curricula and syllabi are not puzzles with one answer yet undiscovered. If *clarity* is sought when a curriculum or syllabus is designed a quality program will likely be mapped out. Any person in religious education can work at clarification from any perspective. Some of us feel frustrated if we have no control of the budget for religious education programs. Some of us lack aptitude for capable administration of programs. Each of us in our present role can achieve greater clarity in the overall process of religious education.

So the reader's expectations will be realistic—this book claims to offer no religious nor educational breakthroughs to any new summits. It is planned only to point to, to urge, to guide religious educators to seek clarity in their endeavors. Only a few topics will be considered. If this book stimulates an appetite for and an appreciation of clarity the reader's attitude will hopefully bring to more topics a critical searching for clarity.

WHY RELIGIOUS EDUCATION?

Religious education is the theme of this book. Probably readers react quite differently to the previous sentence. For some people regard religious education as a luxury—useful but not meant for everybody. Others esteem religious education as a requisite for sanctification and salvation. What is the true value of religious education?

Gnostics, ancient and modern, have held that an elite understand God in a superior way and that their insight brings them God's favor with a cause/effect or stimulus/response necessity. But religious education is one among many human values. It is not a virtue nor a sacred power (sacrament). Religious education, alas, does not confer goodness nor does it enable one to excel in religiously-motivated actions. Faith, hope, and charity are in a category apart from religious education. Accumulation of religious education does not always produce persons characterized by the wisdom so esteemed in the later writings of the Hebrew scriptures. Nor can it impart the charismatic knowledge venerated in the New Testament.[1]

But religious education is more than an optional embellishment for one who has made a total surrender in faith to God. The prelude to such faith, if not the vehicle for faith, is information. A normal person does not fall deeply in love with a stranger. Neither sacred writings nor theophanies function without human agents—be they evangelists, missioners, prophets, interpreters, catechists, gurus, rabbis, or imams.[2] But there is a need to continue religious education after the decisive surrender to God. For the surrender in faith may not endure crises if the person's concept of God is too rudimentary or too vague. Simplistic faith is prone to superstition and to confusion. The normal person hesitates to proceed with great determination if the route is hazy and the goal appears imprecise. Religious education does not lessen the mystery of God and his ways. But hopefully religious education distinguishes God from pseudo-divinities and calls attention to the profundity of his providence.

If religious education cannot bring God to me it can bring God-culture to me. By this is meant the accumulated cult of God—the reflections, responses, and rituals which persons have used to manifest their surrender to God. Just as culture means I do not have to invent the wheel anew, nor discover

1. The elements of experience, acceptance, and faith in the biblical concept of knowledge are deftly sketched in: *Dictionary of the Bible* by John L. McKenzie (Bruce, 1965), pp. 486-7.

2. "The purpose of Christian education is to lead each person into a decision to live as a Christian" says Randolph C. Miller in his excellent *Education for Christian Living* (2nd. ed. Prentice-Hall, 1963), p. 54. Actually this volume does discuss religious education well beyond the stage of deciding to live as a Christian.

electricity, cult means I need not grope for an I-Thou custom-made religion. The fact that "in many ways, in times past, God has spoken to our ancestors (Heb. 1:1)" gives me a tradition to mediate God's actions and human responses to that action, and a critique of the spectrum of responses which have been tried.

Religious education is not faith nor a rival to faith. Its best functions give precision to the concept of God, and clarifications to humans seeking God. Mere goodwill seldom suffices to make any quest successful. Religion is a *way*; directions to orient actions and strong motives to sustain actions are needed if the way is to lead to its goal. When the goal is infinite there is a tendency to be fascinated by one facet of the goal. People with apparently strong faith have sometimes concentrated on a facet to the extent that their preoccupation obscures God (legalism, mariolatry, ritualism are such eccentricities). Intense faith can lead to fanaticism if it is the occasion for neglecting or escaping from other aspects of human living.

So for the generality of believers religious education is a valuable complement to God-given faith. It can prevent religious obsessions; it provides a process for interpreting the faith-gift and the faith-response, and it can help integrate religion with the other aspects of a balanced human life.

WHAT IS RELIGIOUS EDUCATION?

It is with hesitation that the term *religious education* is used in this book. For there is a rather rigid idea often suggested by this term. Implied is the classroom, competitive learning, grading—all the items modern schools use in their efforts to maximize transfer of information. One might question how the Hebrew prophets, Jesus, or Muhammed would react to religious education as it is now practiced.

But no responsible educator can be indifferent to the impact of his message on his students. In a religious education program the student deserves some evidence of success or of failure. The immediate ability to retrieve data is not a very valid indication of success in learning or in teaching. Parents invest time and money in religious education programs for themselves and for their children. They deserve some performance review. Rather than a "grade," based on relative retention and recall of data, more meaningful criteria exist. *Attendance* is often indicative of interest, priority, and responsibility. *Participation* in discussions and activities is a meaningful criterion. *Progress* is the most important item, for seldom do all students begin religious studies with the same aptitude and with the same background of knowledge. It is more likely that a teacher can be accurate in evaluating attendance, participation, and progress than in grading "learning." Religion grades may, in fact, often be measurements either of reading skills or of general intelligence. As children approach adult life more internal processes are at work—curiosity, dynamic faith, and loving empathy for humans in need. Reports to parents and to students should decrease as students mature. But motivation is a constant asset to any learning experience.

Adult religious education courses should not have any feature which might suggest competition or evaluation of individual student's performance by the teacher. Adults have genuine problems for which they hope religion will furnish assistance. They have a desire to fill gaps in their understanding. They delight in the satisfaction which comes from displacing ignorance with insight. They are capable of judging the worthiness of their religious education experience in filling the needs or desires for which they engage in religious education.

But religion is not just an academic discipline; it is a way of life. Jesus protested against excessive stress on knowledge. He stressed love, action, transformation of persons and of institutions. Maybe Jesus would ask contemporary educators about their social action projects, their athletic and recreational activities, about the services being extended to the hungry, thirsty, or incarcerated neighbors. Even "schools" have such adjuncts as sports, music, dances, and extracurriculars of a wide variety. Only "religious education" seems to narrow concern to the space between the students' ears.

On the other hand religion certainly has a prominent noetic element, especially the "Religions of the Book," wherein there is belief that God has revealed truths. Good will, without adequate information and careful thought, can make a person a menace to others. There are times and places appropriate for *learning*. It may be that these times and places need not have bells, parallel rows of desks, and verdicts such as 87% or B+. Religious education may take place on a camping trip, in volunteer programs of care for neglected people, or in a playground setting. It should take place in every liturgy.[3]

---

3. Despite the subdivisions within Judaism and Christianity and the modifications wrought by the centuries, a characteristic design perdures in worship services. There is a liturgy of the Word, a "bible class," followed by a liturgy of the eucharist/sacrifice/"altar call"/communion. The message is taught. Then the congregation responds affectively. For many centuries synagogues and churches and mosques used Readings to clarify faith. The scriptural readings were themselves clarified at times by many types of audiovisual aids: by vestments, candles, cantors and chants, incense, processions, by the medieval miracle, morality, and mystery plays, by instrumental and vocal music, pantomimes, dancing dervishes, mosaics, icons, stained-glass, tapestry, statuary, homilies, "testimonials," and "bearing of

NEED FOR CLARITY

Certainly sketchy ideas will yield to clearer expressions as efforts to improve religious education accumulate. In the meantime let us be open to all ideas, but anxious to prove their true value.

While we humbly acknowledge the values discovered and preserved by those who pioneered in the work of modern religious education we must not cling too stubbornly to their legacy. "Things aren't like they used to be in the good old days"—in fact they never were! The dream of a "catechism" never came true. For humans are always susceptible to ignorance and error. To innoculate people with potent answers to unasked questions and concentrated solutions for future problems were dreams that vanished when experienced in clear daylight. To use words like "catechism" or "CCD" seems inadvisable. For they may conjure up frustrated dreams and fuzzy pedagogy. The gospels do not picture Jesus being anxious that his followers have rote definitions with which to "defend the Faith," especially definitions originating neither in scriptures nor in magisterial teachings of the church. CCD (Confraternity of Christian Doctrine) is an admirable idea—a team of dedicated believers conspiring to pass on the Good News. In execution there has been a beauty in volunteers studying doctrine and methods to sustain and foster our faith. But the prevailing image of CCD is not entirely attractive—a hurried attempt to impose on wearied public school students

---

witness." The educative role of liturgy seems to have declined in most Judaeo-Christian groups. Yeshivoth and Christian schools have come into existence when the readings are in an unfamiliar language or in a dulling monotone or are chosen haphazardly. The scope of this book precludes exploring religious education by means of liturgy. Competent persons are working in this area, but progress is slow.

a condensed parochial school syllabus which was a condensed seminary course. CCD was and is a wonderful concept. But it presently connotes most of what is obsolescent in religious education. For CCD implies a child-centered, amateur, all-inclusive, ultraprecise approach to religion. New trends in religious education cannot be contained in old terminology. The new National Catechetical Directory and the 1977 Synod of Bishops' agenda were in labor to produce worthy offsprings to the programs whose demise is so clearly indicated in *Catholic Schools in a Declining Church*.[4]

This book is not a "how to" manual, in the sense of making teaching a science—a precise method for communicating information. Teaching is much more an art than a science. Each of us has his or her own talent. Picasso is not another Michelangelo. The teacher of ultimate truths is primarily one's self. Gratefully I reflect on many persons who gave me example, data, and methods to know Christianity and some other religions. But the writings which follow are reflections on my own attempts to assimilate and to make clear, meaningful, and integral what I have been taught. The process continues. There will be no endpoint in my being taught religion, nor in my attempts to clarify my insights. At this stage in the adventure I want to tell you how I have pieced together the data of my faith. The effort has brought me much happiness. I hope your efforts will be rewarding too. I am sure you will realize it is *your* effort to clarify *your* faith which will make *our* faith an experience of mutual concern and mutual enrichment.

The quest for clarity is primarily a human effort. It has inherent limitations. As obfuscations are eliminated the dazzling light of faith makes clear the mystery beyond which

---

4. Greeley, A., McCready, W., and McCourt, K. eds. *Catholic Schools in a Declining Church* (Sheed & Ward, Universal Press Syndicate, 1976).

human effort cannot penetrate. God is beyond the cloud of knowing. Moses did not look upon God's face (Ex. 19:9); from a cloud God led the Exodus (Levit. 40: 34–36), attested to Jesus's incipient mission (Matt. 3:17), and accepted the completed mission of Jesus (Acts 1:9). God's revelations are partial, but they are given that we might know him. We have commenced the process of discerning the great Revelation, he who rests on our side of the cloud (Matt.26:64). Great is our misfortune if we exaggerate the confusion in religion (Is. 6:9–10; Matt. 13:14–17, etc.). For we effectively minimize the revelation. History, languages, and cultural differences impose obstacles between ancient revelations and ourselves. But these are surmontable obstacles. Life with its moments of tragedy, ecstasy, and futility clarifies the existence of one more than human who alone can satisfy the human urge for the more than human. Sometimes experiences can be contrived to focus beyond the merely human dimensions of any spontaneously occurring experience. The religious educator's tasks are to design these learning experiences and to prompt reflections also on the experiences beyond our designs. To do and to see beyond the narrow and the ordinary is to grow, to transcend. It is exciting. The educator who fosters these experiences and these insights shares the excitement. The failure to look beyond the limits of time and space (into eternity and infinity) is a failing to grow. This failure induces boredom in the student and in the educator. For both have failed where both sense success is possible. Where there is boredom with religion let us look for confusion. Where there is confusion there is the opportunity and the urgency to seek for clarity. This quest for clarity in place of confusion is the calling of the prophet—major and minor, of Christ, Paul, and all who are called teacher.

My own beliefs and educational experiences are Roman

Catholic. I write from within that tradition. But I hope that the *ideas* will be helpful to religious educators whose *doctrines* may differ. Modern religious education is permeated by ecumenism. So I trust that illustrations drawn from my own religious tradition will be neither confusing nor irksome to any of God's People. The adaptations to various denominations, age groups, and local factors will occur more certainly if *clarity* is pursued, with the educator's eyes on the learners, the consumers, the last link in the elaborate delivery system extending from God to each of his protégés.

If it seems some views on teaching or on content are expressed with excessive confidence, it is well to reflect that I have taught confusedly. The students' boredom and their occasional positive reactions to religious education helped me to find items to discard from my inventory, other items to be reworked, and still other items to be developed with the help of coworkers. Confidence about the future has come from floundering and failing on my part. I have confidence that others can make fewer mistakes than I have made. I share the confidence of many coworkers that a bright era is dawning in religious education. The brightest sign is the quality of teachers. They will draw quality students. Together they will attract enthusiastic support personnel.

1

RELIGIOUS EDUCATION FOR CHILDREN

This chapter is concerned with a child's initial experiences in religious education. The following two chapters concern the religious education of youths and adults. Much of the contents of this present chapter apply to persons regardless of their age. But the child's learning processes have been more extensively and carefully studied than those of his elders. For the initial ideas impressed on a mind uncluttered by memories, associations, and conflicting ideas are easier to study. It seems also that an initial impression is crucial. It becomes the framework on which subsequent ideas will be structured. So, since most people encounter religious thought early in life, religious education for children deserves special attention, both as an immediate experience and as a receptivity for more developed religious notions to be encountered as the child matures.

WATERED-DOWN RELIGION

Religious education frequently conjures up an image of children receiving religious instruction. Why this association of religion with children exists is difficult to explain. For no religious leader chose children for his primary audience.

11

Perhaps, until recent years, *education* has suggested a child-centered phenomenon. Perhaps there is a deep subconscious process at work here. Adults may relieve a sense of personal religious inadequacy by indentifying their children as spiritual monuments who will continue to exhibit the parents' noblest qualities while the parental foibles fade from memory. Or perhaps adults feel ambivalent about themselves as consumers of religion but are relieved if they are at least successful purveyors of religious commodities. If this is true the parents' persuasive powers are most unopposed by their dependent children.

It must be stated unequivocally that religion is misused if it is seized primarily as a tool for control of children. Religion is misconceived if it is understood as a device to smooth or to hasten progress toward maturity. The parallel with the role of spinach is noteworthy. Older people highly recommend it to children for its utilitarian function—it is healthy for children. The presumption is that adults have neither the taste nor the need for it.

Children are astute in recognizing authentic and sincere attitudes. When parents' religious policies for their children do not coincide with their personal practices, not only do children become skeptical about religion, but the general credibility of their parents is weakened. Younger children recognize parental inconsistencies; older children often are strident in their allegations of phoniness.

Disposable religion is commonplace. Once over the adolescent hump, religion joins Santa Claus, jumping ropes, bedtime curfews and other items once so esteemed and so serviceable until the period of growth was attained. This is a very serious problem. It is all too common. It goes by various names—adolescent faith crises, falling in with the wrong crowd, rejection of forced conformity. Whatever is the root cause(s) for apparently pious children becoming impious youth, religious education is suspect as a contributing factor, but also it is a possible therapy.

We cannot conceal our spiritual horizons. If we associate religious education with childhood, children will intuit this outlook and will value religion as an asset for immature people. If adults see religious education as a lifelong process beginning in the childhood stage, then their children will assimilate this outlook.

To imply religious education may have toxic properties will seem outrageous to many people. They will likely extol the values of knowledge and will revel in the realization that probably no generation of children has ever received the thorough religious education that has been provided for twentieth century children in North America.

The effort to provide children with a *thorough* religious knowledge may be the noxious property of current religious pedagogy.[1] Again there may be an anxiety on the part of religious educators, an apprehension that God will check a child's religious comprehension with stern demands. So it becomes urgent to impose on a child some summary of the entire religious tradition. The curriculum is not designed to correspond to the child's level of interest, but to include diluted elements from an entire seminary syllabus. The fact that the teacher is not raising any questions which respond to

1. The classic argument against anticipating adult concerns in the religious education of children is in John Dewy's "Religious Education as Conditioned by Modern Psychology and Pedagogy," in the Proceedings of the First Annual Convention of The Religious Education Association, 1903, reprinted in *Religious Education*, vol. 69, Jan.-Feb. 1974. See also Karl Rahner's "The Sacrifice of the Mass and an Ascesis for Youth," in *The Christian Commitment*, trans. Cecily Hastings (NY Sheed & Ward, 1963), pp. 136–170.

genuine questions in the child's mind is regarded as so much
the better. For a child will not resist overtly nor pose any
objections. Indifference has often been religiously acceptable
to people ill-at-ease with sincere religious discussion. When a
child's critical sense has not yet emerged, educators can make
free use of myths without need to explain mythology or literary forms. Nothing in religion is more quaint than Humpty-
Dumpty or Jack in the Beanstalk. The more bizarre the myths
the more dazzling and memorable children find the lesson.
The instructors find the young child quite receptive to religion, to the realm of the spirit, much like the pristine believers. So many obstacles which adults encounter can be explained away by employing angels or devils in classes for children. The notion of a talking, or even of a visible, spirit seems
consistent to a child, at least for a while. Sometime much later
somebody else will have to "unlearn" the remnants of an inadequate introduction to religion, or if such an unlearner is
not at hand the total religious experience may be abandoned
as a quaint chapter in one's childhood.

But premature exposure to the whole scope of religion may
bring about no evident crisis. The child matures with extreme
religious tranquillity. The apparent serenity has been purchased at a great price, and with great damage to the child.
Let us consider a parallel situation—the urgency which some
people feel to anticipate adolescent interests with intensive
childhood education in sexuality. If the child has learned to
define all the significant terms and to analyze all the actions
associated with sex s/he is informed, but at the cost of evacua-
tion of the mystery from sexuality. Sex can be made boring before eroticism has been felt! Religion can be analyzed, defined, defended in its own recondite jargon before the child
has felt a desire to know God and to surrender to the divine.

As in prudent sex education so in wise religious education it seems advisable to delay giving answers until questions have been formulated. God has chosen not to create people sexually nor spiritually mature. There is a normal, slow progressive fascination with the mystery of sex and with the mystery of faith. We do wrong to cheat a child by depriving her or him of these experiences.

STAGES IN LEARNING

For simplicity's sake children can be regarded as passing through three successive stages. Each of these stages brings to prominence a particular ability of the child and a viewpoint characteristic of that particular stage of maturation. The successive abilities can be termed powers of observation, powers of discrimination, and powers of abstraction. The early years of childhood are marked by insatiable curiosity—to see, to do, to discover sources and causes. The middle years see a child intensify concerns for values, for recognizing right and wrong, good and bad, superior and inferior, altruism and egotism. The child's interests are riveted on heroes and heroines. Sports, movies, science, politics, history, and religion are seen as the arenas where certain persons perform admirably. Admiration is such a child's basic response to human achievement. Only in the third stage is a child delighted to synthesize ideas. As experiences accumulate the child generalizes and classifies. Now s/he is apt to approach reality scientifically—discerning common characteristics amid the many individual things, events, and experiences. Logic, psychology, natural sciences, ethics, social sciences, and theology come within the child's horizons in this third stage.

Let us diagram these three stages:

APTITUDE	ATTITUDE
1 curiosity	wonder / appreciation
2 ideals	evaluation / imitation
3 abstract ideas	understanding

Religious education curricula should not be indifferent to the above schema. In reality one does not make discreet steps from one stage to the next stage. The advancement is progressive. Hopefully the child keeps and develops his early curiosity, refines his hero-worshiping qualities, as he learns to deal with abstract thought. There are incipent anticipations of the latter stages even in the very young child. But educators should capitalize on the current strong-points in the learner's aptitude and attitude.

The concept of God most appropriate to a young (Stage 1) child can be termed Lord of Nature. The birds, flowers, stars, people with voices, eyes, and smiles, space, animals, weather, sunshine and sunsets are fascinating messages from God, perhaps potentially as meaningful as any vision or prophetic utterance will ever be. The concept of God as parent can be learned rather easily at that stage when human parental support is most needed, most total, and most unembarrassingly given and accepted. The unique relationship of this parent to this child may be the paradigm to other relationships of mine-and-thine contrasts, to the notion of property, with its entailed rights and duties. The mystery of creativity as source of both proprietorship and responsibility for one's doings can be grasped at this stage.

In Stage 2 the child normally relates warmly to Jesus. If the child while in Stage 1 balanced authority and affection (Lord and Father concepts) in Stage 2 he will maintain a similar balance between Jesus/Friend and Christ/Lord. The human and the divine will not be incongruous if the child regards Jesus Christ as both brother to himself and as child to the divine Father.

In Stage 2 the primary source for contact with Jesus is the bible. But the relationship of Jesus to the parent- or Father-God requires familiarity with the Old Testament, while the relationship of Jesus as friend to the present generation entails familiarity with the sacramental mystery, with the replication and diversification of Christlike qualities in lives which share and prolong the Christ-life—with the holy people or so-called saints. It is paramount to situate the "historical Jesus" in the process enshrined in the Old Testament and extending into the postbiblical or ecclesial era.

The final stage of childhood is the appropriate time for the child to relive the community's history, with its various confusions, reflections, and clarifications. These tensions brought about definition, precision, and sometimes divisions. Only when a child's mind can be at ease with the past and with anticipation of a time yet-to be will development have interest for the child. Only in the light of controversies and misunderstandings will the value of precise terms be recognized, and only then will authoritative pronouncements to resolve conflicts be esteemed.

The diagram on the following page can be amplified:

CONCLUSIONS

Looking at this scheme may suggest some modifications for curricula designs. The polemics, the preoccupation with definitions, the dogmatic, the doctrinal creeds might well be delayed until the personal aspects have been well-grounded. The scheme seems inconsistent with some currently common catechetical methods, but very consistent with salvation his-

APTITUDE	ATTITUDE	NOTIONS	SOURCES
1 curiosity	wonder/appreciation	father Lord of Nature	nature community: family, neighborhood, etc. creativity; property
2 ideals	evaluation/imitation	Jesus: friend Christ: Lord Jesus Christ: brother & son saints	bible sacraments
3 abstract ideas	understanding	doctrine Holy Spirit	history: the community's reflections

tory, and with the process whereby the Trinity was revealed or apprehended by our ancestors.

The foregoing analysis is in no way intended to lessen attention given to religious education for children. Rather it urges maximizing the educative experiences of children. The proposal calls for patience, for adapting the contents to the child's psychological and pedagogical readiness. Hopefully the key ideas will be learned more profoundly and with greater appreciation. Rather than a veneer of countless religious data the child will grasp deeply the relatively few key data, as a skeleton or substructure to which can be attached the secondary and dependent elements. A child with a rich insight into the basic relationship of Parent, Friend, and Spirit is in a favorable situation for integrating any other religious concepts into a coherent way of living with God. The activities of God (forgiving, giving, guiding) flow reasonably from the triune roles of authority figures in the child's own family.

The program for gradual religious education is a challenge to faith. An eight-year-old child who has received the traditional exposure to the whole spectrum of religious faith and traditions will appear much better educated than the eight-year-old child whose religious education has been primarily an in-depth communing with nature and its Lord, along with experiences of community with its ramifications. The product of traditional catechetical methods will have an impressive command of the religious jargon—able to speak of sacraments, scriptures, revelation, inspiration, church, episcopacy, papacy, etc. Naturally these concepts will correspond to a child's powers of conceptualization. But in faith there is a presumption that the slow, careful, deep, person-centered, experiential, in-process technique will bring a child to an ever-awakening sensitivity to God and to our relationship with God. The product of the traditional pedagogy may have a difficult time in stretching childhood concepts to correspond to adult perceptions. If the concepts are too inflexible they will be discarded, with or without more mature replacements.

The proposed process tries to utilize effectively the strong points of each stage of a child's development. But the early aptitudes do not cease. Religious educators should try to prolong the curiosity and idealization into adult life. Otherwise closemindedness and agnosticism displace the desire to know and the drive to imitate what is most attractive. Faith suggests religious education should seek to facilitate adult living with attention to the religious dimension of life. When faith is relatively weak the quest for tangible, measurable results becomes prominent. Such education will seek to produce child-phenomena, young people in whom are deposited vast religious erudition, children who can define technical terms, eg., transubstantiation or hypostatic union. The urge to see results usually brings about stress on memorizing, on facility with the in-group vocabulary, and the result is an isolation of religion from the other areas of human interest, with a consequent dual personality in the student. Religious education will then seem quite remote from life on the playground, in the family room, and from the concerns of geography and science classes. There is a questionable leap of faith demanded of the traditional educator—to believe that the child fortified with answers will be able to cope with questions which arise in later years. But it takes an act of extreme faith in the educator's foresight to believe that the future questions can be anticipated and that appropriate answers can be instilled in students. Today's answers may be inadequate for tomorrow's questions.

Probably one becomes a mature person only by passing through childhood. The mature believer is one whose religious education was progressive, and was not from a premature imposition of an adult outlook into a child's mind. "The kingdom of heaven is like a seed planted . . . ". Eventually the child should encounter the total parts needed to fill his religious horizons, but it is difficult and discouraging if all the parts overwhelm him before their individual values are perceived.

The long, patient exposure and experience of God from Abraham to Paul suggest that a slow, carefully-designed religious education for children will obviate the difficulties so distressing to those now in youth ministry. For if built-up boredom is the climax of a child's religious education neither progress nor retreat seem possible in the postchildhood years.

2

RELIGIOUS EDUCATION FOR YOUTH

As one reaches the peak of mental and physical development life stretches out in all directions, with all varieties of enticements. *Expectancy* is the attitude of youth.

Concerned adults observe how avidly young people react to rock music, action-filled movies, and to the romantic myth of "feelin' free in the Pepsi generation." It seems resonable to presume religious educators can strike a responsive note, can generate youthful enthusiasm, and can expect satisfying results from their work with youth.

Attention, effort, and budget should reflect religion's concern for and expectations from youth. But *restrained expectations* are advised. Authentic religion is not like soft (or hard) drinks, or current movies, or sense-shattering rhythm of noise and strobe lights. Religion is not a titillation of feelings, nor a method to dissolve persons into impassioned peers.

OBSTACLES

No other religious educator lives in the twilight of faith in which those who work with young people grope. Reflection will reveal reasons for this difficult restraint of expectations. Three reasons will be sketched—each with a consoling aspect.

First, the majority of youths whom religious educators in North America encounter have been overexposed, overdosed with religion in their childhood years. Usually adults and children are at least neutral in their emotional set toward religious education. But too many young people from conscientious families come to high school/college/young adult programs with an aching hangover. They are at rock-bottom, intoxicated, and are aware that now is the time to fight free from addiction to whatever is "the stuff" this zealous "pusher" is promoting so energetically. There are so many other new avenues, new products, new learning experiences. For many, the normal quest for novelty is gratified by a taste of natural and/or social sciences, modern or ancient languages, cars and cosmetics, highly organized athletics, debating, band, chorus, dramatics, travel. But high school religion classes look like and taste too much like they did in Grade 8 and Grade 7 and forever. Given the steady diet of religion before it is relevant the high school student arrives at spiritual obesity. The victim of the process is the religious educator of youth. The consoling feature is that a more patient explication of childhood religion will eventually lighten the task of those responsible for religious education for adolescents. Jesus felt the same frustration—remarking about his fruitless attempts to patch something new on a too-familiar, threadbare garment.

Secondly, teenagers are in a time of turmoil. They are skeptical, if not antagonistic, toward authority in any form—God, teacher, institution. They are developing a personal code of values, but this usually means a distressing hypercritical phase. Self-acceptance can be strengthened by their stressing the hypocrisy of others. A healthy dependency comes easy to children. Interdependency is a joy to adults. But those caught between childhood and maturity lean clumsily and reluctantly on either younger or older people. A wise old bishop revered for his dedication to all that is authentically Christian once advised me that if many young people kept some contact with the Christian community during their adolescence he judged our programs to be successful. Total alienation is so easily provoked at a time when people are called to walk on the ridge between dreams and disillusionments. There is consolation in the fact that being a teenager has a built-in escape. Eventually adolescence is outgrown. Awkward and often obtuse personality traits are smoothed out into attractive, stable, friendly, controlled interpersonal relationships.

Thirdly, among youths individuality is emerging with frightening strength. Conformity and sensitivity to peer-group pressures may mask the crisis of self-acceptance. As in no other decade of life are the needs of normal people so divergent. Religious generalities are rather ineffective in this transitional stage. Personal experiences are so diverse. Psychological growth spurts are so different within any group of young people. Attempts to use religion for therapy are as dangerous as doling out one prescription for a class of ailing students. Here the religious educator must take consolation only in faith. The Holy Spirit does not abandon nor despair to bring teenagers toward the many mansions Christ has fitted for them in their Father's home. The task of meeting the many obscure needs of each member of a youth group is beyond the possibilities of the educator. In humble faith it ought to be affirmed as beyond reasonable expectations.

TEMPTATIONS OF EDUCATORS

The trauma of passage to adulthood is an experience each of us is asked to endure only once. But religious educators sometimes are vicariously agonizing and writhing over the metamorphoses of their proteges. There is a beautiful quality called empathy. But there is a diabolical process called temptation which must be opposed in this context.

Thus a religious educator may suffer severe anxiety because a young student choose to take a sabbatical from formal religious education. Then the teacher will likely become judgmental in an area of mystery. Religious education is not like breathing—an interruption is seldom fatal. The ease with which a youth can exit from formal religious education usually determines the ease of reentry when obstacles to learning have been outgrown or out-manuevered. Many are called at the sixth hour, the ninth hour, or the eleventh hour. Some respond early, take a siesta, or wake up to find God's call is still a summons, not a dismissal. Few people find religion so pedestrian that it has the same meaningfulness every year of our lives. Sometimes one must step back and try to face life without religion, or parents, or friends, or money, or God, or polite manners in order to discover the real (not the reputed) value of these assets.

The second temptation to which religious education personnel are prone is falsification. In the effort to make religion for youth innovative we may present pop psychology, pop art, literature, music, movies, TV, or sociology and call it religion. High school religion courses built around the juke box fads of six months ago, around Jonathan Livingston Seagull, transactional analysis, movies with English subtitles, the current rise in violence/CB radios/macrame/etc. are probably mislabeled merchandise. Religion is never made relevant by making it diluted to the point of disappearance.

Falsification occurs quite subtly when a well-meaning educator begins (and ends) "where the students are," with free discussions on how the students feel and what they may be thinking. Adolescents are quite susceptible to narcissism. Fostering self-centered monologues is not religious education. For a free-wheeling rap session seldom zeroes in on religion. A theistic religion is never learned by mere introspection. A "rap session" can be a prelude to group interaction. Ongoing "rap sessions" relieve a teacher from preparing and teaching while the students are liberated from learning.

A comprehensive youth program within a church congregation will include recreational and social events. But legitimate recreation, even if sponsored by a pious organization, is not rightly termed religious education.

The last falsification to be mentioned is the purchasing of popularity by the religious educator. Each of us has some charisma to dazzle some young people. We can improperly enhance our drawing power by overuse of popcorn, soft drinks, excessive flattery, and playing the role of an overaged teenager. Concessions should be made to individuals, but to those in need, to those likely to derive a religious benefit from manifestations of extra effort.

STRATEGIES

The ever-growing "how to" literature on youth programs tells of what has worked in one place at least once. But only occasionally does it seem that these successes are replicated elsewhere. So the continuing output of success stories only proves that what takes root in rural Iowa seldom grows well in metropolitan Boston. There follow a few sketchy ideas which seem sound and their potential success has to be established by trying them in various places with varying groups of young people.

Programmed-instruction[1] packets are successful if they are

1. Programmed-instruction is an innovative method to individualize learning. Basically it divides a lesson into small, definite sequential items. Each student separately studies an item, is tested on that item (usually by

carefully prepared and are used by convinced, skilled teachers. As yet there has not appeared marketed programmed-instruction courses in religious studies. But learning centers, placement tests or inventories of religious information, and lower teacher/student ratios are building the substructure for this promising development in education to be utilized in religious instructions.

The recent realization that mature spirituality can and has developed from numerous educative experiences has stretched the syllabus for religious education for youth. The *essentials* need not include every preoccupation which interested ancient, medieval, or contemporary students of religion. Ecumenism is not just a luxury item for those who have mastered so-called rudiments. It can yield a fresh insight into the center of Christianity, especially for those who live in a religiously pluralistic society. Morality can reach the core of faith if it is not a simplistic study of items whose value is universally recognized—truthfulness, honesty, sexual control, etc. Practical people are likely to be interested in the ambiguity of moral judgments in the total context of evil mixed with the good, the better, and the best. Discernment of the Christ-like way for me to act in this context, with my limitations is moral experience which develops intimacy with Jesus by the realization that the Spirit of the risen Christ animates sincere believers. Praying, psalms, religious art, architecture, journalism, literature, parish and diocesan programs are neglected areas but hardly secondary in significance.

---

electronic or mechanical devices) immediately after s/he has studied it, receives an instant report of his performance with a correction of any misconceptions. When a block to further learning is detected the student is routed through an alternate presentation of the difficult item. Each student progresses at his own pace. Criticisms of programmed-instruction are plentiful: the solitary defense is that it works well.

A ridiculously easy way to multiply options for religious education for those on the verge of adulthood is to open to them enrollment in adult religious education programs. For youths can be challenging, broadening partners in dialogue with their elders.

The service aspect of religious formation is strongly urged by the American Catholic bishops.[2] It can balance the too cerebral stress in much of current youth ministry. But "doing good" is not easily fostered. In a group not everybody has the readiness to enter upon given projects of service. The group can pull along borderline individuals by sustaining motives through periods of personal discouragement. Confirmation is often an apt occasion for presenting the spectrum of service to youth—from the mundane chores in the kitchen and garage to the glamorous tasks in hospitals and orphanages. The wise religious educator will strive to associate religion with service, by stressing motives and models. Confirmation does mean being a doer, a giver. Small steps can begin a growth in the role of service. Large steps imposed suddenly can make it even more difficult to begin the altruistic service characteristic of a mature religious person. The same cautions about sensitivity to individual readiness and to the real or imagined difficulties are called for in designing retreat experiences for youths. The reluctant participant will likely gain little, but will drain much from the spirit of others in the group.

Creativity will give a freshness to religion. Teenagers, long overexposed to television, educational films, and to other audiovisual resources, are at the appropriate age for role-playing based on biblical incidents or on moral dilemmas. Debates, "press conferences," writing and acting original skits, composing parables and psalms, producing a slide show, or an 8-mm.

2. *To Teach As Jesus Did* (U.S. Catholic Conference, 1972.)

sound film can challenge the imagination of the students. Not only will they likely gain more than a superficial grasp of the incident being studied, but by translating the "message" to a different era or culture they will discover the relevance of the original event or teaching. A youth group can learn teamwork by producing a brief film or filmstrip to clarify the "message" of a gospel section, to explain a sacrament to a non-Christian, to introduce a stranger to the local congregation, to fantasize Jesus speaking to the local parish, to a high school assembly, to the state legislature, to other subgroups within our society. As by-products teamwork is developed in such projects, art and religion are united, students rather painlessly pass from *hearing* about religion to *saying* something about religion, and to *using* religion as a critique of current mores.

It sounds so platitudinous to urge patience as a promising teaching tool. But it is impossible to produce instant adults. The great doctor of the church, St. Augustine, left us some prayers from his youth: "Let me be for a little while. . . . Give me chastity but not yet."[3] One often must simply wait. The collegian who comes home for vacation often discovers the home parish liturgy is intolerable, the homily is an insult to her/his intelligence. But the graduate might realize that the college chapel had a very homogeneous group, whereas the parish has a real catholic mix of ages, occupations, and levels of learning. Many a freshman critic-in-residence later recognizes the responsibility which comes with education, and on graduation humbly adds her/his talent and training to the parish community.

Since faith is a virtue it seems safe to urge religious educators to have greater faith in youth programs. But excess in virtue is a fault. Too many aspects of adolescent religious

3. *Confessions*, VIII, 5, 7.

education are left in the realm of faith. There are no standardized tests to measure effectiveness of the learning process, nothing like College Entrance Examination Board scores for religious studies. There is a presumption, in faith, that years of enrollment in many courses, always with the latest textbooks, and with expensive supportive apparatus, are producing religiously literate youth. Inventories of religious information (objective tests of one aspect of religious education) have always dismayed me by showing the extensive erosion of the religious information so carefully presented to children. But, in faith, we can counter by saying religion is more than information—it is attitudes, or virtues, or a way of life. There are instruments to measure these criteria too.

There is the lingering difficulty in isolating the contribution of formal religious education (rather than family, liturgy, peers) to the attitudes and actions of young people who have been exposed to rather extensive efforts in religious education. It takes no faith to recognize the expressed or implied *boredom* which religious education has impressed on many young people. In faith, one can listen to the faithful and can expect to hear the Spirit of Christ. At this time, in our country, presumably conscientious parents are content to see their teenage children terminate formal religious education. The young people, presumably in good faith too, frequently say, "Enough—religious education is not for me at this time." The parents and youth are the church, and they are addressing us. In faith we should accept their judgment: religious education as it is usually found is unacceptable. There is a tremendous task of rethinking and revision to be done. Trying to do tremendous tasks makes life interesting and worthwhile. It makes faith become alive and active.

When much has been tried and much has failed the religious educator must not presume personal failure has occurred. Before starting all over again it is wise to call time-out, and to meditate on "Hope: Foundation of Religious Education" in Gabriel Moran's *Vision and Tactics* (Herder and Herder, 1968, pp. 98–110). Understanding teenagers is the theme of several booklets by James DiGiacomo, S.J., eg., *Questions Young People Ask about Jesus and the Church* (Claretian Publications, 1973); *We Were Never Their Age*, with Edward Wakin (Holt, Rinehart and Winston, 1972). Books and articles by Richard Reichert and by Michael Warren treat religious education for young people. *Five Cries of Youth* by Merton Strommen (Harper & Row, 1974) centers on the youthful consumers of religious education.

3

RELIGIOUS EDUCATION FOR ADULTS

New personnel among religious educators often shiver in fear at the prospect of designing adult syllabi or teaching adult groups. But if prudent, adequate effort is made the adult response will be gratifying. For this group appreciates the opportunity to learn. Moreover there are grounds for presuming the impact on adults will filter down through their dinnertime conversations and coffeebreak discussions to reach families and friends.

THE CONSUMERS

Prudence suggests beginning with the consumer. The adults are not just overaged children nor ex-youths. The adult educator must seek new methods and resist the habits which may have been developed in teaching younger classes. Adults have already had their sense of wonder stimulated, have already resolved the common moral and emotional crises, and have developed powers of communication. So much of the traditional teacher's job is already done.

Adults may be diffident in entering a formal learning situation. Years may have passed since they were students. Lingering deep in their memories are the trappings of school—rows of desks, grades, standing to face stern questions. Prudence suggests a fresh, light, relaxing approach. The site, the availability of refreshments, and soft lighting can deinstitutionalize and humanize adult group learning experiences. But a casual disregard of start-and-end-time irks many adults. Certainly with an adult group competition in religious performance is out of place. At least some of an adult population will want an input into the selection of topics. In any case all deserve to be consulted and their preferences respected. Proposing tentative topics prompts an important array of decisions by the prospective learners. Later some remarks will be made on matching topics with the adequacies of the personnel. But here prudential guidelines can be sketched.

Obviously intelligent people will not make a commitment to adult religious education per se. But if a variety of topics can be offered, at a variety of times (weekday/weekend, daytime/evening), with an honest "course description" (including fees, name of text(s), duration of sessions, and of the entire series) intelligent decisions can be made, and specific interest need not be worked up at a later time. The "course description" is a map; it tells where we are going and by what route. It will prevent wandering off on side roads and up blind alleys.

Adults tend to be pragmatic, experienced in dealing with problems. It is unlikely they share the professional religious educator's fascination with global topics, such as church, faith, theology, Christology. It is noteworthy that the religious educator is likely to feel superadequate with specifically religious topics, but prudence suggests the consumer is not likely to buy religion in isolation from so-called secular interests. Seldom do adults feel any need for a new ecclesiology or Christology. The challenge they face is to integrate smoothly their faith and their other vocational interests. Very few adults want an escape from present reality into religious education. So interdisciplinary materials are appealing because they are useful. Speculation on esoteric elements is a luxury few adults will afford. They feel no urgency to become familiar with any particular book from the bible, although key biblical themes are intriguing because they are real parts of life today. Very few adults have religious nostalgia. The deja vu of a "refresher course" is usually a letdown. Adults, like any person, enjoy freshness, discovery, grappling with the yet unknown.

Usually adults are at ease with contemporary terms, and uncomfortable with the religious jargon of decades past. The well-intended device of favoring the terminology of years gone by is disconcerting to adults who wrestle with problems for which the old answers seem inappropriate. The fresh, contemporary adult ways of speaking about religion are easier for pursuing learning than are the ultraprecise terms long ago buried in a child's ideological vault. Mature persons can accept the ambiguities and imprecisions which are genuine aspects of the sacred mysteries.

Adults whose formal education has been interrupted years ago will readily resume the techniques of learning. But their horizons may have shrunk. The educator's task often is to sketch the big picture for self and for the others—rethinking familiar concepts, consequently reshuffling priorities, redefining the meaning of being a believer.

The educator of adults has less reason and less right to stifle wild conjectures or apparently radical attitudes. Usually the educator can presume a "party line" response is familiar to the group, whether it is accepted or is considered an insufficient response. Polarization and ongoing debates are seldom educative experiences among adults. Adults have experienced the realities of life. If some have developed variant interpretations and definitions of "faith," "religion," "church," "hope," etc., their views merit respect. Hopefully an educational program will bring about some changes in personal views. But scorning, scowling, and scaring will likely entrench maverick views. The science of religion, theology, develops when individuals part from the group to think what was heretofore unthought, if not unthinkable.

Since so many details on prudent adult religious education vary from place to place it seems wise to design a brief checklist or attitude-survey to ascertain if the topic, time, duration, text, publicity, fees, format, depth, participation opportunities, teaching aids, locale, furnishings, and leadership were good, satisfactory, poor, or very poor.

THE EDUCATOR

Each religious educator must find his or her own adequacy—by evaluating background, available time, and resources. But one need not teach only what one has mastered. There is something refreshing for all concerned if one can resist the stereotype of *teacher*. Beyond the requisite competence in the general area of religious knowledge, a catalyst or leader or facilitator or fellow searcher need only structure and sketch the problem to be investigated, make available the resources, control the research process, exploit the group dynamics, even play cheerleader at times. If the religious educator is not threatened by this less lofty role, the entire group is relieved of pressure. The seminar is the model for such a group. But the seminar director or leader does not resign responsibility—s/he keeps a hand on the pulse of the group lest moods or tangential interests obscure the delight in pursuing useful knowledge. The educator at ease in the seminar model will be more successful if s/he does not dress more formally than the others, does not sit apart from or raised above the group, uses first names if the others do. Such an educator is quite content to let others teach the entire group. No pretense need be made at mastery of the topic. If one brings the religious dimension to a topic or problem fascinating to the group s/he fulfills an essential role. Adequacy means accepting the limits of one's knowledge, while recognizing and utilizing the wealth of experiences and backgrounds brought by the group members. But the effective educator should know how to advance or how to prolong a discussion, how to heat up or to cool down a conflict of opinions.

Adequacy does not mean bringing the group to a figurative plateau, but rather to start with them up a slope. For continuing education is an achieving process, not an achieved education. So the syllabi should be open-ended, the learning stimulated but not terminated, the curiosity aroused but not satisfied.

Time for remote preparation is a critical factor in developing adequacy. It may be possible for an energetic educator to work up an interdisciplinary study. But it may be overwhelming if one starts with no background in science or psychology or arts and then delves into the study of Teilhard de Chardin or transactional analysis or liturgical music. For such programs may attract people skilled in these areas, even though they have limited experience in bridging the gap between their profession and religion. Team-teaching is likely to upgrade the adequacies in such situations. In some circumstances the religious educator functions most adequately merely as a resource person—eg., in a physicians' group discussing ethical questions, or in a Parent Effectiveness Training group.

Adequacy of library resources, appropriate audio-visuals, and resource persons should be surveyed before developing a possible topic for adult religious education.

Adequacy of an adult program should not be judged by sheer numbers of participants. The infrequent big-name guest lecturer will draw crowds. The shock-therapy of colorful iconoclastic religious martinets will appeal to the sizeable group which is responsive to a dazzling answer-service approach to teaching. But the passivity at the learned lectures and the confusion from the glib, detached master tend to be caricatures of the prudent, adequate religious educator.

These rather random remarks on adult religious education are no substitute for adequate groundwork. Various nuclear ideas of Malcolm S. Knowles (*The Modern Practice of Adult Education*, Association Press, 1971; editor of *Handbook of Adult Education in the United States*, Adult Education Association, 1960) have been applied to religious education by Leon McKenzie in *Adult Religious Education* (Twenty-Third Publications, 1975). The sociology and psychology of small groups' interactions are analyzed in a vast growing body of publications.

As in any relatively new field there is an expectation that new developments will abound in adult religious education. Communication networks are just beginning to function. Recent increase in TV violence and other kinky experimentations suggest commercial television may be going the way of the moribund movie industry. Bowling, bar-hopping, saunas, spas, complex stereos with pulsing lights may also be cresting, and may be beginning to induce ennui. The leisure explosion may soon reach the fallout stage. Then will genuine, worthwhile, challenging, educational adventures become the mature person's leisure and luxury. Religious learning will likely fill a more significant role in confirming adults in their true adult role. For what is at stake is one's own identity. If to say "I'm a Christian" is only a mixture of formalism, confusion, and willingness to be defined by some other vague party, then one's life is unstable and may shatter under stress or tragedy. Faithful *followers* seldom became saints. Presently they seldom remain viable members of the Christian community. In the future informed believers will give vitality to the community and will be the material from which God will likely fashion saints.

4

TEACHING HOLINESS

The following chapters consider some general topics which occupy a prominent place in religious education programs. These topics may be taught as specific courses, or as units in a more extensive course, or merely as points alluded to briefly in a study of some related topic. In these chapters there is no attempt to adapt the topics to the three levels (children, youth, adults) considered in previous chapters. The adaptation is necessary. But it cannot be done remotely. Somebody familiar with the students must make the adaptations. For these adaptations will be not so much in light of the chronological age of the group, but in relation to the experiential background, previous learning, and level of interest of the group members. *Holiness* is the initial topic to be woven into religious education programs.

Holiness means acting rightly. Preliterate people, whether young children or adults in a primitive culture, have no clear concepts of virtues or of perfection. But they do conceive of actions and of persons as right or wrong. Ancient Israel figuratively both stood in awe and ran in pursuit of God because he was and was doing right at all times. For others too God was the standard, exemplar, and source of right living. So Old Testament writers called God holy, and God's people were termed holy. The New Testament called Jesus the Holy One of God, and his postresurrection influence was termed the Holy Spirit, while his church was called a holy people. Holiness, acting rightly, is more than ethics. It is thinking, doing, being, or becoming right. Morality means following the mores, the customs, of society. Holiness means following the divine one who is consistently and uniquely right. God's parental affection and guidance were regarded as right and holy; his wisdom, power, poise, judgments, faithfulness, penalties, forgiveness, revelation, and delegation of responsibilities were described as *right* by the biblical writers. In creating humans in his image and likeness God gave a destiny and a calling to holiness.

Occasionally people preoccupied with religious education must remind themselves that religion is not an educational enterprise. Formation is the goal, not just information. Unless any educational or pastoral endeavor fosters holiness it is merely a distraction from pursuing the ultimate goal of both human living and of religion. So any valid religious education is engendering at least some opportunities for holiness. But the centrality of holiness in both life and religion merits a specific study of holiness within any thorough religious curriculum.

The above paragraph does not seem controversial. Yet it can generate uneasiness. Recently a religiously-affiliated university asked me to offer a course in the department of religion. A course outline was submitted, required textbooks were selected, and the title Christian Holiness appeared at the top of the outline. A few days later the dean, department chairperson, chaplain, and I had lunch together. They mentioned that the curriculum committee had approved the proposed course, the contents, and the textbooks. But the dean and the department chairperson shared the committee's alarm about the proposed title for the course. They thought it would appeal only to the odd students, that it did not sound academic, but rather that it sounded emotional, and that it did not seem related to the other courses currently offered in the department of religion. The chaplain suggested the title be Christian Lifestyles; this was acceptable to the administrators.

Probably these administrators know the students' mentality very well. Perhaps holiness is regarded as freaky, as emotional rather than intelligible, and as only remotely related to the rest of Christian wisdom. If so, there are fundamental misconceptions to be faced by the teachers. In teaching a positive, doctrinal course these misconceptions will be encountered. In affirming the genuine tradition, the errors will be gradually corrected, in an indirect, nonpolemic way.

What follows is one teacher's approach to this topic. There is no presumption that it is superior to any other person's strategy. But it is an example, possibly helpful to a teacher who has not yet formulated any personal plan to teach holiness. So it should be examined critically as one among many possible presentations in this area of Christian education.

STARTING POINT

Every course and each unit in a course should begin with a question characterized by clarity, and by a pragmatic value. These two qualities mean that answering the question will be interesting and desirable on the part of the class. The key question to open exploration of holiness is: what is the Christian idea of "the good life"? Equally important is the question: how is holiness or "the good life" attained? Every society has a vision or goal known to its members, a concept of "the good life." Staunch Communists can tell us what their concept of "the good life" is. So can racists, hedonists, socialists, and social scientists. So ought Christians to grasp clearly what

Christ, the highest authority on Christianity, had in mind as "the good life" for himself and his followers.

The first subordinate question is: how do I find the idea that was in Christ's mind? An open discussion will likely yield a firm consensus that the gospels, the rest of the New Testament, and the ideas expressed by those Christians most apparently attuned to the spirit of Christ will be the most reliable indications of the "good life" as conceived in the mind of Christ.

The next question will be: *what* is found *where* the thought of Christ is preserved? Depending on the students' familiarity with scriptures, doctrine, and hagiography, and also on the time available some loosely guided group research and synthesis will yield conclusions somewhat like these:

> Jesus esteemed intimate friendship with his Father as a paramount factor in "the good life";
>
> Jesus gave high priority in realizing the "good life" to Christlike service to fellow humans—caring for them and curing their troubles according to various circumstances;
>
> Jesus saw that responding to the influence of the divine Spirit is an essential for "the good life."

Since each of the above statements requires more careful consideration, a brief sketch of the three ingredients follows.

FRIENDSHIP WITH GOD

First, Jesus stressed the personal, with God as the center of religion. Neither law, wisdom, temple, abstract virtue, nor ritual was the heart of man's spiritual life. Jesus never regarded God as unknowable. He believed God had revealed himself to the unlearned (Luke 10:21; John 17:3), that God's preferences are knowable to us (Matt. 7:21; Mark 14:36; Luke 11:9–13). In the Sermon on the Mount (Matt. 5–7) it is clear that Jesus did not regard scriptures as the apex of human familiarity with God. Jesus truned to prayer, not to biblical exegesis as he prepared to choose his disciples, to commence his ministry, before the transfiguration, and before his betrayal/arrest/death. Because Jesus regarded prayer as functional, praying had priority over action. Busy persons seldom conclude, "I'm too busy to eat," but they realize only a healthy, energetic, well-fed person can sustain an active, productive life. Praying was energizing for Jesus. Moreover praying before making major decisions indicates that Jesus regarded prayer as a two-way communication, wherein the mind of God was manifested to the praying party. It is not easy to translate affirmation of Jesus's prayer program into an imitation of his deeds. But history suggests that the mystics are the decisive people, the achievers, the ones with orientation amid confusion and inertia. History suggests that anybody who has ever taken this world both seriously and sympathetically has looked beyond this world. The social doctrines, the love ethic, and the winsome personality of Jesus are not fully embraced by those who remain agnostic about the one whom Jesus called, "Abba, my Father." To love tremendously one has to experience tremendous love. Jesus related concern for the human condition to God's concern (Matt. 10:29–31), preoccupation with needs to God's providence (Matt. 6:25–34), building community from obtuse elements to God's actions (Matt. 5:44–45), and ascribed to God the driving force for human progress (Matt. 5:48). In general it seems the praying of Jesus shows distinctive characteristics: the absence of complaints which are so frequent in Old Testament prayer

texts, the absence of specifics in petitions to God, the awareness of possible deceptions in our requests (cf. Matt. 7:9–11),
and a mix of liturgical prayer, spontaneous praying, traditional
verbal formulas and innovative forms.

The insistence on *Father* will likely undercut a perennial
question about holiness—is it God's work or our task. Hindu
gurus ask if the model is the cat or the monkey—the kitten is
carried passively by the jaws of the parent, while the monkey
must actively cling to the abdomen of the parent. The question is crucial—if holiness is God's work it need not be our
concern. If it is our task then pursuit of holiness becomes the
path to self-destructing pride. But a Father preexists his
child, initiates dialogue with his child in the language of the
Father, and the child learns to speak by witnessing the
Father. Yet the genuine Father respects the child's freedom
(Luke 15:11–32) and individuality. A loving parent influences
a child profoundly but does not determine the child's free
decisions. A loving child exerts responsibility by responding
to the parent's communication and anticipations.

CHRISTLIKE SERVICE

The second conclusion about the expressed thoughts of
Jesus was that Christlike service is part of "the good life"
advocated by Jesus. Many people met Jesus. None remained
neutral in attitude toward him. One way or another each one
realized that he cared about them. They could not be indifferent. They reacted—with loving enthusiasm for him or with
passionate hatred against him. Caring means Jesus did not
simply accept people as they are. He wanted their potentials
developed, their weaknesses strengthened. Curing means
Jesus took the role of enricher in people's lives. Often curing
means listening as people uncover their real problems and

devise their strategy to meet the problems. Sometimes a smile, a visit, a pat on the back can be genuinely curative.

SPIRIT-LED

Thirdly, responding to the divine Spirit is part of the "good life" advertised by Jesus. Profound though the influence of Jesus was on his associates, they were a small number in a small region of Asia during a small span of time. As his earthly life drew to a close, Jesus gave a promising message—a Spirit of Truth, a Helper, would be sent. The Spirit, like the wind, was free from the bonds of time and space. The Spirit would give what is needed. Jesus built on the Old Testament tradition of divine Spirit. The decisive leaders (kings, priests, prophets) were Spirit-led people. Dry bones from a cemetery could be led by the Spirit to life and to coordinated action (Ezek. 37). Discernment of the mysterious Spirit was the believer's task. In particular holiness means discerning between means and ends, between the real and the phony, between the holy and the very nearly holy. The Spirit is not a God "up there" or "out there," nor a God beside us or before us, but a divine power within us, enabling our minds to grasp truth, our hearts to receive and to reciprocate love, and our senses to communicate truthfully and lovingly.

A subsequent question will likely occur to students: what is the significance of each of the factors usually associated with holiness? Five factors can be considered. There is no logical order for studying these factors, except that three of them (prayer, meditation, action) correspond to the trinitarian theme above—intimacy with the divine Father, service in the style of Christ, and acceptance of the leadership of the divine Spirit. The two more inescapable factors, personality and obstacles, might be considered initially.

PERSONALITY

Definitions of personality abound. This suggests the idea is of general interest, but that precision is difficult to attain. Obviously each of us is equally human; we have the same human nature. Yet each of us is distinct, individual, different. Each of us has unique fingerprints, voice patterns, and a certainty that we differ from others so much so that we never confuse self with anybody else. What influences form this personality? Heredity is universally recognized as a determinant of personality. But genetic influence may be less significant than is commonly thought. Siblings, even identical twins, are quite dissimilar in personalities. Parental influence is probably due more to nurture than to nature.

Despite books and courses, self-development of personality is probably very limited. The ambitious person who disassembles her or his components in order to rebuild a better model may parallel the person who takes apart a Chinese puzzle with the plan of refitting the parts into a new design. The taking apart is rather easy; the effort to reassemble is likely to be frustrating. Anybody who would make effort to transmute his personality might reflect on his outlook. He is implicitly critical, resentful about reality, disappointed with a gift, anxious to escape from the ever-present self. Acceptance, rather than rejection, of one's identity, seems the starting-point for gracious development of personality. There is no shortcut to satisfaction with one's personality, only the inevitable path from potential to reality.

Faith is challenged not to ask God to exchange our personality for some other design, but to believe what we have is a gift carefully chosen by a concerned parent with infinite resources. We are free, but our ability to alter our personality package is quite limited. But we are free to act in the light of our self-knowledge of our potentials.

People do influence personality. Cultures, parents, and peers are the three strong influences from people. Each culture surrounds us with its goals and its taboos, without consulting us. Society imposes on us a language, a style of art, a form of government, a philosophy of education. These elements do shape our personality somewhat. Parents' influences seem to be stronger when there is no intention to form personality in their offspring. Perhaps parents place a child someplace along a mythical spectrum extending from "very secure" to "insecure." Security/insecurity concerns two aspects of life: self and surroundings. A wise parent challenges a child to surpass self and to relate to the environment. But an overly challenging parent can make a child consistently disappointed. The child who never seems to measure up to parental expectations acquires a guilt complex. Usually this sense of failing is transferred by the child to his outlook on God. The overly-protective parent cautions the child about the pitfalls on all sides—germs, dangers from accidents, viruses, possible falls, fires, fights. Inevitably the child regards himself as surrounded by a hostile world, threatened by all other people, yet this is presumably a bad world made by a so-called good God. It is likely that on meeting others the child will have resolved to hurt before being hurt, and to meet God with distrust for the many boobytraps hidden throughout his creation. Guilt about self-worth and anxiety about environment are the insecurities every parent transmits in some fashion to every child, and which every child must wrestle with in clarifying his concept of God, the ultimate parent and source of all personal and environmental imperfections. Key peer influences can be reduced to "putdowns" and confirmations. In terms of transactional analysis we are convinced by others, "I'm OK" or "I'm not OK." It makes a tremendous difference how we are accepted or rejected by others, for we tend to introject and to ratify their judgments.

A simple classroom demonstration can be made by dividing either floor space or wall space into four quadrants, marking the axes with placards:

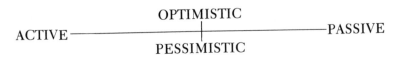

ACTIVE ——————————————————— PASSIVE

OPTIMISTIC (top)
PESSIMISTIC (bottom)

Any personality will fit someplace on the scheme illustrated. It is well to clarify the meaning of the terms by eliciting synonyms, eg., *active* implies energetic, dynamic, aggressive, a doer, competitive, impatient, hyperactive, lively, while *optimistic* suggests cheerful, pleasant, smiling, sunny, easygoing, hopeful, sanguine, confident. Then a student volunteer is asked to place beyond the limits of the axes cards indicating excesses of each characteristic. These cards read: LAZY; DEPRESSED; FRIVOLOUS; AGGRESSIVE. Another student (or pair of students) is asked to match locations on the diagram with the personality-types on these cards: VIOLENT CRIMINAL; SUCCESSFUL SALESPERSON; DISCOURAGED; WHITECOLLAR CRIMINAL; DROPOUT; DREAMER; ARTIST; EXCITED; BORED; WORRIER; BITTER LOSER; POLITICIAN. Another student is asked to consider the attitude toward others characteristic of personalities in each of the quadrants, and to place these cards in the appropriate quadrants: LEAVE ME ALONE; ADMIRE ME; LOVE ME; FEAR ME. Finally a student will be asked to ponder how others see personalities in each of the quadrants, and then to place these cards in the proper quadrants: SWEET; CHARMER; DULL; TOUGH. There follows a guided group discussion on "which group in the diagram has material for holiness?" and " which group has obstacles to holiness?" The discussion ends when there is a consensus that each personality has possibilities and problems related to holiness. The teacher then stresses the importance of knowing one's personality, of realizing where on the diagram one is situated. Then it is important to accept personality and to act in respect to one's personality. Our freedom does not extend to gross alteration of personality, but rather to act freely in the light of our self-knowledge. Prayerful familiarity with the words and actions of Jesus can yield an honest self-awareness from which can be constructed a strategy to utilize personality assets and to counteract personality flaws. Each quadrant represents humanity, a capacity for holiness. The teacher should sketch implications deriving from an absence of self-knowledge: reliance on customs, crowd sentiment, public-opinion polls, the behavior of "average Americans," or of "typical Catholics" as guides for decision-making. Unconsciously advertisements, movies, fads may become surrogates for personal decison-making.

The student has hopefully been brought to appreciate self, and to esteem his or her personality as a precious gift, and to realize that a human person is the only, genuine, authentic, guaranteed representation of God on the market! There are limits to our ability to change (Matt. 6:27). Students can be asked to imagine God coming into the classroom. Would any ask him to change his personality? If so, might he simply hug the person, and say nothing. If so the student might get the message: I love you as you are. I made you *you*!

The student should be led to evaluate the significance of these items for holiness:

intelligence / slow learning
education / ignorance
wealth / poverty
talented / ungifted
long life / brief life
health / sickness

The conclusion is not simply that these factors are irrelevant. They are aids or hindrances, depending on one's reactions to these raw materials.

Throughout the study of holiness, excessive introspection is to be avoided. It is important to know where *others* are in the quadrants and to deal with them accordingly. Paradoxically we have surprising freedom to modify the personalities of others. As a "significant other," in particular as a parent, we can engender a sense of security, a realization of "I'm OK" or we can transmit diffidence, anxiety, guilt complexes, and fictitious self-images to those close to us.

OBSTACLES

The real and imaginary obstacles to holiness include sin, ignorance, fears, and humiliation.

There is surprisingly little unanimity about the concept of sin. Two prevalent but diametrically different views can be summarized:

Sin is everywhere—this view seems to have been held by Augustine, Luther, Jansens, Puritans, and by antisecular believers today. It is common among guilt-ridden people. It implies angelism, the possibility of holiness by withdrawal from as many worldly, contemporary, social, economic, political, technological, intellectual interests as possible.

Sin is nowhere—this view tends to characterize the outlook of Rousseau, humanists, psychiatrists, some prison reformers, many women's lib devotees, some ecologists and evolutionists. Here again angelism is prominent. For irresponsibility is rather easily established by such rationalizations as:

"The devil made me do it."
"We're products of our times, of the environment."

"Everybody is doing it."
"I'm confused."
"It's as traditional as apple pie."

A precise concept of sin is: a choice of creature over the Creator. A less abstract concept is: whatever lessens love—of God, of self, of others. A clearer concept: whatever intentionally lessens human life, ie., human freedom and responsibility. A contemporary concept: whatever knowingly impedes personal development. This last concept fits practical situations realistically. For it is rather apparent that the strongest God-given drive is to develop—acorn to oak, tadpole to frog, human to person. The addict is not free to develop a career, nor free to keep society's rules, nor free to make choices about use of money, time, or talents. The pornography consumer is not free to pursue other forms of recreation, not free to develop three-dimensional, live, person-centered, love-centered sexual interests. Compulsive drinking, eating, smoking prevent development of maximum health potentials. The student who habitually "goofs off" in school will not develop power to make intelligent choices, in place of acting on instincts, impulses, and prejudices. This is not a radical nor innovative concept of sin. For the Mosaic commandments indict those who fail to develop as humans (aware of their origin, destiny, and proper relationship to God), and those who fail to let others develop (by disregarding authority, hostility, seduction, theft, deception, and possessiveness).

Ignorance is often a real obstacle to holiness. People with good will are hampered by misconceptions and prejudices. Often one aspect of Christian holiness is confused with the totality. A secondary devotion or a single virtue obscures the whole complex. Fanaticism often ensues, or simply journeys on tangents rather than progress toward Christ as the center of Christian faith. Holiness always comes with an uphill effort.

A fuzzy idea of God, self, and of holiness will be incapable of engendering sustained uphill driving force. Without sufficient knowledge indecision is inevitable. If one cannot make informed decisions or if he permits others to direct his freedom completely there is minimal virtue and vice in his life.

Fear is an obstacle if it is neurotic or inappropriate. Each of us is an imperfect offspring from imperfect parents. So we accumulate our own insecurities concerning ourselves and our surroundings. These fearful characteristics are not obstacles to holiness, if they are recognized, accepted, and woven into strategy to utilize their latent potentiality to be assimilated into our human development. To deny them or to surrender to their force is to compromise our opportunity to advance toward holiness. For a guilt complex often leads to scrupulosity, and anxiety often leads to phobias. Both of these ailments tend to paralyze progress. A self-centered concern for holiness often produces acrophobia, a fear of releasing our grip on mediocrity, of being different from the majority of people, of surrendering to the mysterious divinity. In general it can be said that insecurity complicates giving and receiving love. But complications are the raw material for maturity.

Humiliation is a very elastic term. It overlaps with others among the obstacles already considered, eg., insecurity with its fears. By humiliation is meant opposition to one's healthy aspirations. In the pursuit of holiness humiliations are painful and unwanted, even though they have value. Their value stems from the fact that humility is the condition for advancing in holiness. For a satisfied person must be made hungry, an upright person must be humiliated—*humus* is the Latin word for earth, soil, ground. In humiliation God can reveal himself, can reveal our dependence, can destroy our pride, and can deepen unity and love—the stuff of holiness. To perceive God in focus, a human (also from *humus*) must look up.

So we must find ourselves where we are—far below God, in need for him to reach down to us. Temptations are a type of humiliation; they must not be grouped in the type of obstacles to holiness called sin. But past sinning or forgiven sinfulness is in the category of humiliation, not in the class of real obstacles called sin.

Briefly these other obstacles also deserve mention. Lack of support or loneliness handicaps the pursuit of holiness. In our inconsistencies we can be buoyed up and drawn forward by others who are not victims of a desolate mood. In the Garden of Gethsemane Jesus asked first that his companions pray with him, then pleaded for them to awaken and wait one hour with him. Excessive pain is a genuine obstacle for it demands attention on self and thus prevents concentration on any other interest until the source of suffering is dealt with. Self-centeredness or excessive introspection is a distortion of reality, a confusion of values, a falsification of priorities, and thus an obstacle to holiness which comes from truthfulness and altruism.

Having considered personality and obstacles, the other three factors to be summarized are prayer, meditation, and action. They are primarily relationships to Father, Son, and Spirit.

TEACHING PRAYER

Praying was a paramount interest of Jesus as he is depicted in the gospels. Jesus engaged in liturgical and "private" prayer, group prayer, recitation and singing of psalms, and original prayers. He cautioned others about long prayers and about ostentation in praying. Sustained prayer at times entails difficult praying. Sustained prayer is possible if one has a clear concept of God.

At first the concept of God does not strike students as so very important. Here are some techniques for giving emphasis and urgency to seeking a clear concept of God. Turn to a student and say, "tree," and then to another student and say "tree." Ask each if she or he understood what was said. Then ask each if she or he thought of a large or small tree, with leaves or with needles, alone or in a forest. Both heard the same word; both have a true mental picture. But they have differing pictures. Then say to a student, "God," and to another student "God." Develop the possible differences in concepts and possible sources for divergent elements in the two mental pictures.

Gregory Baum has sketched two contrasting but valid concepts of God in current thought:

Lord of the Universe   *Life of the World*

Lord of the Universe regards God as lawgiver, "king of kings," father in heaven, creator of the world, while Life of the World affirms God is love, truth, Word, Spirit. Lord of the Universe is more traditional. It tends to isolate church people and non-church people, to isolate sacred and secular interests. It regards religion as a pull away from the earth, while it looks upon the church to bring God's friendship to the world's people. Life of the world affirms that God is found in all people, as "light of the World." God is discovered in business, recreation, government, and social life. Life is seen as the bearer of God's friendship, while the church is to proclaim and to celebrate life with God present. Both concepts retain the essence of Old Testament theology—that God is real, personal, friend, and with influential power. But these diagrams might suggest the differences in the two concepts of God in relationship to our environment:

Lord of the Universe:	GOD WORLD	: :	sacred secular

Life of the World:	$\begin{smallmatrix}&&&D\\&&L\\&&R\\G&O\\W&O&D\end{smallmatrix}$	: :	secularreligious

It is well to recognize that these two concepts of God which have been summarized are encountered quite often. It is wise to recognize our own concept. It is noteworthy to consider what exclusive concentration on the transcendence of God implies, and what exclusive concentration on the immanence of God implies.

A second teaching technique, role-playing, will prove effective if the unique "teaching aid" is available. Three large name cards are prepared in advance, each with a loop of string to go over the head of the participants. The cards read: GOD   YOU   YOUR PARENT. A live infant, wearing the card YOU is brought into the class and each student puts on the GOD card and holds the baby for a few minutes. The teacher poses questions to those who hold the baby, such as:

What do you want for him? ("All I can give him.")

What do you expect from him? ("A smile.") ("That s/he accept what I offer.") ("Nothing.")

What do you want him to do? ("Develop who he is.")

What is his name? ("Whatever his parents choose.")

What if his parents wanted a dark-haired girl? ("Too bad.")

Now the students take turns wearing the YOUR PARENT card, and holding the baby who now wears the YOU card. The teacher asks: Can you drop him on the floor? Can he be choked? Do YOU realize this? What does it say to us if YOU fall asleep in YOUR PARENT's arms? Does YOU realize his vulnerability and incapability of making his own way? Is your role as GOD much different than your role as YOUR PARENT? Is life a "trust walk"? Such a technique will hopefully pinpoint these elements in the Judaeo-Christian concept of God: Father, trust, dependence, surrender, providence, mutual love consequent to mutual respect.

If the concept of God is accurate and vivid, the teaching-learning-practicing of prayer is inevitable. There is a limitless opportunity for the teacher to explore God mediated by symbols and communal responses appropriate to these various aspects of the divinity. The scriptures provide such themes for prayer: God as Father, Creator, King, Judge, Wisdom, Word, Spirit. The teacher can show God as reflected in art forms, from the prayerful folk-art of the catacombs, through the classic cathedrals and chorales, to contemporary collages and celluloid slides/films. There are plentiful resources to aid the teacher in arranging these media for stimulating prayer.

PRACTICING PRAYING

The effective educator will always be one who has labored to work through solutions to the problems presented to the students. Holiness should not be a detached *subject* proposed in a neutral fashion, even though the educator may choose to avoid autobiographical data. An effective salesperson is one who endorses a product s/he esteems. The religious educator presumably has and continues to work with his personality, against obstacles to religious growth, to be a pray-er, familiar with Jesus, and attuned to his Spirit. Since praying seems to be the touchstone for these various efforts, a few pages on the educator's praying is in order.

One pedagogical suggestion likely to stimulate little controversy and even less interest is a recommendation that religious educators pray. Such a proposal is not exactly breaking new grounds. But if somebody should ask "why" or "how" then ideas might come into being or might become clearer.

All persons, all programs, all learning aids, all budgets, all committees with their agenda, minutes, reports, by-laws, and subcommittees exist to foster holiness. But holiness is God's business, a divine gift. Amid brainstorming, buzz sessions, and bibliographies one should not overlook a requisition for divine aid, a shared decision-making process involving the Holy Spirit, and some consulation with Christ about Christlike simulation exercises.

It is not enough to affirm that holiness is the ultimate goal of our efforts and that holiness lies within God's area of influence. The speculative awareness becomes an operative principle when prayer becomes a part of every stage in lesson-planning.

To the extent that a religious educator is habitually aware that his work is in the field of faith he perceives new dimensions to his labors. He will presume his efforts are helpful, even though immediate results are not cause for wild elation. He will believe the Lord can bring about benefits other than those which he anticipates, that indirectly people other than the students can be enriched by his struggles, and he may, in dark frustrating moments, be buoyed up by the realization that *he* is perhaps the chief beneficiary from his educational efforts.

Prayer will clarify and solidify a teacher's identity—both positively and negatively.

Positively, the teacher is a follower of Christ, whom the gospels most frequently term *Teacher*. He is to be charismatic, for teaching religion is a gift from and of the Spirit of Christ (1 Cor. 12:28; Eph. 4:11; etc). Like Jesus, his best lesson planning begins with prayer (Luke 6:12–13; 9:18–20; 9:28–36; 22:41).

Negatively, a religion teacher's prayer helps him to realize he is not God, nor a parent to the students, nor a policeperson, nor Santa Claus. The teacher cannot and should not try to impose faith or pass judgment on persons. The teacher can be the occasion for grace, a vehicle for revelations to reach hearers, and a stimulus to thought. But the teacher's role is a humble one. The Trinity gives life, reveals divinity, and inspires holiness. The teacher's relationship to students has limits. The teacher must limit intrusions into various areas of a student's life—tastes in clothing, preferences for hairstyles, choice of leisure-time pursuits, etc. The teacher should manifest refined manners, and the teacher may personally appreciate a student's polite decorum, but the teacher cannot expect a few hours of classroom contact to offset the behavior patterns observed or tolerated at home. Capabilities and ideals differ—teachers must be patient, hesitant to play foster-parents or to try patching-up what is judged to be poor parenting. Similarly, a teacher's true role is primarily instructional. Preoccupation with posture, grammar, chewing gum, and general tidiness is an abuse of authority and a misuse of the opportunity to teach. Lastly without prayer a teacher may subtly turn to the cult of popularity. A person hungry for human appreciation and affection can buy a reasonable facsimile by abdicating leadership to the whims of the students, or by trying excessively to gratify the students' tastes for trivia.

Since teaching is both a noble and a humiliating task it is vulnerable to both disastrous pride and deadly discouragement. Prayer brings God into focus, preventing pride, and prayer draws our attention away from self, remedying the despair born of human frailty.

Lastly, one speaks of praying with a unique authenticity when one has prayed before speaking.

MEDITATION

Meditation is an awkward word to designate familiarization with Jesus. The Evangelists did not write biographies of Jesus, or merely factual, descriptive accounts of some episodes in his life. They compiled Good News. Meditation, rather than reading, will disclose the Good News about Jesus.

It must be a patient process, sifting the attitude of Jesus from accounts of various events, separating the reality from its symbols, being open to clarification and rectification of first impressions. Holiness comes about when we are "turned on" to admire, imitate, to make his priorities our own, to let his outlook become ours, to internalize the mentality of Jesus much as we assimilated the language and customs of our parents, so that in unique, unforseen events we will react without any immediate plan but as Jesus would react because his ways of living have been indelibly impressed on our thinking and evaluating processes. It sounds very theoretical or poetical, but if one has met a truly Christlike person he then understands and esteems meditation. Eventually Jesus acts so as to become for me clearly "the glory of God (John 1:15)," the masterpiece of God's creative art, and my brother in the most real, significant, enriching way.

ACTION

Action is the test of sincerity in concern for holiness. For holiness is not an intellectual exercise. It is a way of living, not with rare heroic deeds, but with habitual quality in doing everything we do. Jesus stressed action—"not every one who says 'Lord, Lord' shall enter the kingdom—not every tree brings forth good fruit." When asked "Who is my neighbor?" he asked "Who acted as a neighbor?" The obstacles to holiness are very often obstacles to action—ignorance, fear, peer pressures, self-centeredness. Courage, wisdom, and prudence can activate the person immobilized by these obstacles. The classic example of such activition is the Pentecost event narrated in chapter 2 of Acts of the Apostles. A diffident, uncommunicative, inward-directed huddle of eleven men became the Apostles who changed the world. The Spirit of the risen Christ is action-orienting, but Spirit-directed action is subsequent to patient, discerning, decisive cultivation of the Spirit. That Spirit is found within us to confirm our actions. But also the Spirit is in the community—and my contemplated actions should always attend to the Spirit's apparent influence on the church. A later chapter of this book will discuss the church as a topic in religious education. So no development of this manifestation of the Spirit will be made at this point.

CONCLUSION

Like any Christian mystery holiness entails the total mystery who is Christ. Essential to understanding holiness is belief that Christ redeemed us, that despite our weakness, inertia, disorganization, the power of the risen Christ can penetrate, rectify, beautify, and sanctify us!

The teacher might anticipate some of the questions which follow: Is holiness evident? If the answer is no, students will likely think the topic of holiness is merely conjectural, imaginary, an ideal confined to the mind. Is holiness rare? If the answer is yes, students may consider the topic does not pertain to ordinary people. Ordinary holiness is meant to characterize the ordinary Christian; extraordinary holiness is found only in extraordinary people. But the subject of holiness fascinates everybody whose religious concerns are more than superficial. Only cynics have lost all remains of hero/heroine-worship which is so noticeable in every normal child. Is holiness an art or a science? Like all fundamental human activities, holiness is both an art and a science. For there are God-given aptitudes or predispositions which can be developed, much as a musician or artist uses innate talents. But there are art academies, music conservatories, and instructions in which accumulated wisdom and experiences inform students on methods to exploit talents efficiently and thoroughly. Is non-Christian holiness different? Inferior? More difficult? Perhaps these are speculative questions, like any comparative estimation of degrees of holiness; perhaps there are no satisfying answers, only speculations. It may serve to open discussion on the role of scripture and church in fostering holiness for Christians and on any surrogates performing similar functions for non-Christians. Are there recommended texts? Any Christian writing other than the bible is only a commentary or explicitation of the biblical message. Never should any of these subsequent writings obscure the primacy of scriptures. Merton's *Life and Holiness* and van Zeller's *Sanctity in Other Words* are worthwhile readings to relate the biblical teachings to contemporary life. But other people are comfortable with classics, such as *The Following of Christ* by Thomas á Kempis or *Introduction to the Devout Life* by Francis de Sales, although they should be read critically and as products of their era. Michel Quoist and Louis Evely have written various small volumes for contemporary readers, but they must be read in the context of modern European problems and preoccupations. People with a theological bent find writings of Dietrich Bonhoeffer (*The Cost of Discipleship*; *Letters from Prison*, etc) tell of holiness in the anxieties of modern life and with the modern existential categories of thought.

5

TEACHING BIBLICAL MYTHS

Christians and Jewish religious educators look to the bible as a sourcebook, a norm, a help and sometimes as a hindrance to their work. Attempts to bypass scriptures have usually failed because God became lost in the process. Attempts which truncate the bible into salvation history or into messianism or into moralism either leave the learners with an unbalanced religious view or dependent on some secondary source(s) to give an integral religious view to the learners.

But to contemplate "teaching the bible" is much like planning to "teach the library" or to "teach knowledge." For the scriptures are an anthology, compiled over a period of centuries. There is much history from a religious perspective, pious anecdotes, prayers, fictitious and true stories with and without literary quality, by simple and by sophisticated writers, the esteemed wisdom of a people, the diatribes of their political and social critics, the scandals of those in high places, the virtues of those in low positions, depictions of heroes and heroines with their adventures and achievements, the formation and struggles of two communities (Israel and church). In the light of the whole bible, the religious educator's task is to select elements which are nuclear, ie., key parts to which other scriptural data can be assimilated at various times under other circumstances.

Rather arbitrarily, three elements which are inescapable in religious education for children, youths, and adults will be explored in this and the two subsequent chapters. Again a caution is advisable: the degree of sophistication of the students will vary over a wide spectrum. So the educator must, by prior knowledge of the students, or by administering a survey, be aware of the initial attitudes and awareness brought to the study by the learners. Age or years in school can be deceptive criteria in establishing a starting point for a biblical study. The elements to be considered are teaching biblical myths, miracles, and morality as summarized in the commandments mediated by Moses.

THE PROBLEM

When a teacher presents the alphabet to a class it is unlikely that any student will offer resistance to the content of this particular lesson. No alternative seems more appealing; no letters seem inappropriate; nor are there any suspicious sounds among the vowels and consonants. But religious education does evoke varying degrees of hesitant acceptance, the questioning of some items, and the dubious fitting of other elements into a satisfying totality.

It may be that today's students, well trained in the natural sciences, bring to their religious studies a mental set so keen and rigid that they immediately resist the traditional Good News, wisdom, salvation history, and law from on high. The thorough teacher probes this barrier and deals pedagogically with the obstacles encountered. A sketch of this probing and response technique applied to the teaching of biblical myths is the content of this chapter.

Often literary classics fail to interest a class. It is easy to say that the acknowledged work of art is not on trial, but that the students' tastes are being judged and found faulty. The presumption is that the classics contain a universal message. But the students must decode that message, then encode it so that it says something meaningful to their unique situation. To hold interest, information must be relevant, data must resonate with an existing interest or must respond to a genuine curiosity aroused by the problem presented in the story. *Vicarious experience* has very limited appeal to students—"How would you have deployed your legions if Vercingetorix was on the left flank and the Gauls were running low on supplies?" The fact that generations of students have studied Caesar's *Gallic Wars* is an insufficient recommendation for today's youth. *Perennial value* does not convince students who avidly read the late edition of today's news and then wrap tomorrow's garbage in it. Often the magic names (Shakespeare, Sacred Scriptures, Socrates, etc.) arouse expectations which are not fulfilled. The *eye-opening discovery* on first reading the bible or *The Aeneid* or *The Divine Comedy* is certainly the exceptional reaction. The more common initial reaction is a realization of quaintness, of contrast between the preoccupation of the classic writer and our contemporary quests.

The bible poses epistemological problems for today's students. "It all seems so unscientific" is a quick (and accurate) judgment. "One can't tell how to separate the figurative language, fables, and faith." "It's too long and complicated," which is the critique usually rendered on first hearing Beethoven or reading Milton. The problem in religious education centers on myths.

MYTHS AND MYTHOLOGY

A literary myth is an element in a mythology. The mythology of a people reveals that society's root values and aspirations. The myths are stories which depict reality in a grand, heroic, extreme way. The mythology of ancient Israel was the transcendence of God and the wisdom in loving surrender to his proffered covenant. The myths comprising this mythology included Abraham's willingness to sacrifice his son, Job's fidelity to God amid his overwhelming distress, and the Suffering Servant Songs of II Isaiah. The mythology or network of myths preserves and transmits the élan of a culture, facilitates an individual person in his finding his place and his potential within his culture, gives a basic insight into the totality of the culture's concern (*Weltanschauung*), and subtly gives a feeling or affectivity for the prime values upheld within the culture. The American mythology includes the eagle, Fourth of July fireworks, the Battle Hymn of the Republic, and the genocidal "winning of the West." Of course the word *myth* is sometimes used less precisely, with the connotation of unreality ("mythical two-headed monster") or falsity ("the mythical rising and setting of the sun"). It is difficult to think of a literary myth as true or fictitious, much like a landscape or a symphony is not judged to be true nor false. A quality literary myth corresponds to and illustrates the corporate self-image and ideals within a culture. Myth has been called a public dream. A dream is not a reality, but reality is the sequel to a dream pursued.

THE CONTEXT

Perhaps the word *myth* is an ill-chosen name to designate scriptural communication arts. But the term is in possession and careful definitions abound, definitions designed to prescind from misinterpretations and misconceptions. It is possible to avoid a precise definition—thus avoiding a shaky basis for a very important understanding of divine revelation. The term "package" is imprecise, flexible, familiar, adequate, and it does not force one to premature judgment of truth or falsity.

A few propositions seem to follow: abstract, esoteric topics have more mass appeal when pleasantly packaged. Profound truths must be packaged carefully if they are to be delivered to people of limited vocabulary and of insufficient metaphysical concepts. A rather prosaic product can generate sales appeal if it is made exciting by its package. But biblical writers and the divine Inspirer were anxious to "sell" ideas, to generate interest and commitment by use of humor, emotional appeal, suspense, surprise, and artistic beauty. The packaging is of supreme importance. Who taught us (and our ancestors and presumably our descendants) basic morality and psychology? The old Greek Aesop did, packaging fundamental truths in stories enacted by foxes, hares, ants, etc. Catastrophe was first pondered in terms of Humpty-Dumpty's disintegration; the Old Woman Who Lived in a Shoe posed for us the problem of responsibilities exceeding one's coping powers. Jack and the Beanstalk analyzed for us the role of perspective in evaluating both conflict situations and assets.

Packaging can transcend barriers to effective communications. If one recalls the funniest joke s/he has ever heard, and then imagines its impact on one's grandmother, on an African bushman, or on the U.S. Senate, the favorite joke may not seem inevitably, universally laugh-inducing. But Walt Disney's cartoons packaged humor which entranced the most primitive tribes, delighted the most sophisticated people, and rejuvenated the adults while maturing the children.

Generations of children have had their feelings hurt, have suffered from toothaches, and have observed the death of plants, animals, and persons. They have asked their parents *why*? The elders have answered but never adequately, for the mystery of evil remains enfolded. But no parent has responded more impressively than the desert sheiks around their campfires who told of a snake suggesting that people play God and act independently of God. Death, pain, fatigue, fratricide, and lust followed. Operas, stained-glass windows, dramas, paintings, and literary scholarship have used the paradise myth as their theme. In many languages, in varied homes parents tell their children of the fall of Adam and Eve when children wonder about a good world that is not so good.

If packaging ideas is first considered in the broad category of a communications technique, students can treat the phenomenon without the emotional trauma they associate with the vehicles employed to transmit our saving faith doctrines. In complete objectivity they can reflect on and recognize that they once had unquestioned faith in prosperity following upon blowing out *all* the candles on a birthday cake, that celestial beings reacted favorably to a tooth placed under a pillow. Without tranquilizers, chain bolts, and watchdogs, small children doze off peacefully, assured that a guardian angel is on nightly duty to repel intruders, extinguish fires, and repulse goblins. Christmas gifts were understood by sensible people to originate in the polar regions and to be delivered obviously by reindeer via chimneys. The students can usually recall how they "outgrew" these Santa doctrines—the parents who had propagated the beliefs told them it was otherwise. With a little guided reflection it becomes clear to students that their faith was faith in their parents' faith. For a statement by the parents sufficed to identify Donner, Blitzen, and teammates as fictional. A concept of providence usually causes the role of guardian angels as once sketched by consoling parents to be revised.

Students can laugh at their former faith in traditional folktales. That faith was not shattered, but was merely outgrown or revised.[1] The folk-wisdom mediated by folktales is

---

1. Moreover, maturing minds usually pass from faith in the faith of their elders to a personal relationship to the object(s) of faith. As one's own wealth of experience accumulates s/he relies less on the collective wisdom and testimony of the older generation.

still cherished, but with deeper faith. Experience has confirmed belief that decisive, strenuous effort in moving forward is usually beneficial, and somehow blowing out all the candles was an effective illustration of a principle later to be demonstrated by less contrived life-situations. The satisfaction of giving without our generosity being acknowledged is a basic Christian experience (Matt. 6:3–4). The vision of the whole world being blessed with unsuspected benefits from a mysterious origin associated with the birth of Jesus is a succinct theology of redemption. Adolescents often will laugh at their former naiveté about Santa Claus, but they hesitantly realize that *they* will utilize Santa Claus to reveal Christian values to their own children. They will not propound divine providence, but rather guardian angels, to convince their children to sleep peacefully. The students do not consider use of these traditional teaching devices to be deceptive. They insist they will not lie to their children. Yet they have no illusions about the Tooth Fairy, about hovering one-on-one angels with wings, nor about the bearded benefactor in the red suit driving the sleigh. From personal experience it becomes clear that packaging is a necessity, that packaging conceals the contents, that packaging material is distinct from the contents, that the same contents can be packaged in different ways according to the circumstances of delivery, that mature people do not evaluate the contents by the appeal or the distaste occasioned by the package.

THE VALUE

The more profound the reality, the more likely it will be packaged in myth. Human affectivity has been deeply explored by modern sciences, but the Valentine merchants still market heart-shaped cards with pictures of Cupid with his bow and arrow to summarize *falling* in love. The most dispassionate area of knowledge is likely electricity. Yet it abounds in mythical terms: current flowing along wires, particles attracting particles, substances resisting flowing currents, and invisible electrons rubbing off some rugs on some occasions onto some shoes.

With a healthy respect for purposively packaged ideas students are well-disposed to deal with myths which abound in all religious teachings, especially in scriptures and their reflection in sacred art. When this difficult lesson is completed, the student usually finds the mystery still remains, for one who tries to demythologize usually discovers he has merely remythologized. But the student will have learned what the package contained and will have used her or his own creativity to repack and communicate to another the mystery within.

Hopefully a careful effort to deal with students' distrust of mythology will yield a clear perception of the enshrouded mystery to the students and satisfaction to the religion teacher.

As myths are unpacked they are best assembled into the complex called a mythology. Then the relevant question arises—does this coherent complex of myth/stories express an insight and a yearning which I can call my own? The believer will answer yes—I know it; I see it. Others will recognize it reflects accurately the mind and heart of the biblical people.

6

TEACHING BIBLICAL MIRACLES

The previous chapter urged educators and students to deal with biblical myths *outside* the context of faith. No appeal was made to a principle of inerrancy nor to divine inspiration nor to official interpretations of isolated texts. Now the topic is the miraculous element in scriptures. Again the effective educator is cautioned not to try to terminate investigation of a real problem by dicta such as "you must believe . . . you may not question . . . it is part of the great mystery."

THE PROBLEM

Few modern Christians or Jews seem totally at ease with the biblical accounts of miracles. There may be several reasons for this discomfort: education in the sciences presumes the absence of the miraculous; sudden cures are suspect because of experience to the contrary; modern glib evangelists often prey on simple folk by stressing questionable healing powers. It may seem psychological malfunctions are remote from faith and morals, that miracles detract from the religious themes of the scriptures. Bringing relief to a few ill people, praiseworthy though it be, seems an achievement incommensurate to the redemptive task of turning the whole world around.

The New Testament records of miracles seem more disturbing to Christians than do the accounts in the Hebrew
scriptures. Perhaps it is easier to interpret the bizarre events
(Moses and plagues, Elijah's exploits, Samson's escapades,
Daniel's escapes) as folk legends appealing to the forerunners
of the modern readers of comic book adventures. Perhaps the
Christian believer shies away from gospel miracles because of
a subconscious aversion to Docetism and Monophysitism.[1]
For Christians the problem of miracles is focused on those
related in the canonical gospels.

THE DATA

A few of the gospel miracles are maverick, atypical. Finding
a coin for paying taxes by looking in the mouth of a fish (Matt.
17:23–26) may be simply a little in-joke among the disciples
and their intimates. The water, bread, and wine miracles (eg.,
Matt. 14:22–23; 14:13–21; John 2:1–11) have an obvious illus-
trative role in expressing sacramental doctrines. But the more
common, the typical miracles of Jesus are cures involving
three types of maladies: the blind (eg., John 9:1–49), the lep-
ers (eg., Mark 1:40–45), and the paralyzed (eg., Luke 5:18–
26). The cures are consistently related to faith and morals by
the dialogue between Jesus and the party being helped.

THE INTERPRETATION

Certainly blindness, paralysis, and leprosy were maladies of
relatively high incidence in the area where Jesus lived. But
the gospels show Jesus was preoccupied with the epidemic

---

1. These two early errors led the early councils of bishops to issue creeds
to give precision to the genuine Christian traditional belief about Jesus.
Docetists looked upon human nature as something shameful. So they con-

personality problems of people. The *unawareness*, whether the causative factor is ignorance, prejudice, or insensitivity, is the universal blindness which Christian faith claims to alleviate. The *ugliness*, whether projected or introjected, that isolates persons from persons, is the leprosy which makes all of us build asocial, defensive quarantines. *Inaction*, whether from diffidence, ambivalence, or delayed execution, is the universal paralysis which Jesus sought to exorcise. What happens to one (or two) men as Jesus entered (or left) Jericho (Matt. 20:29–34 and Luke 18:35–43) is not so consequential to our generation as is the impact of Jesus and of the Christian way of life on my obtuseness and on my inadequate vision of God and of his revealing creation.

Since religious educators cannot verify historical data about any of the gospel events termed "miracles" or "signs" by the Evangelists, caution is advisable in presenting these pericopes to students. Extremes are to be avoided. One such extreme is a naive acceptance of the text without any interpretation, or with a simplistic rationalization—"God can always do as he wishes," or "the unexpected is to be expected when a man is one with God." Another extreme is to present a limping explanation dependent on a naive hypothesis that there is one literary form called Gospel Miracle which is comprehensive and consistent. Some of the startling events in the gospels are not in the genus with the curing episodes. "Miracle" should be used in a restricted sense. The theophanies (at the birth of Jesus: Luke 2:13–15; at the baptism of Jesus: Luke 3:22; at the temptation crises: Luke 4:1–14; at the transfiguration: Luke 9:29–32; at the death of Jesus: Luke 23:44–46) may

cluded God's Son only seemed to be human, and only appeared to have human limitations. *Monophysites* stressed the divinity of Christ so much that they spoke of the humanity being absorbed into or dissolved away by the overwhelming presence of divinity. So for differing reasons these two groups did not conclude that Jesus Christ is "true God and *true man*."

be pedagogical devices, much like the halos, rays of light, and cupidlike cherubim added to the reality in pious works of art. Cosmic phenomena are a figure of speech commonly used in illustrating peak experiences. Luke found the celestial disarray pictured long before by the prophet Joel an apt way to express the profound internal gift of faith given at Pentecost (Acts 2:17–20) and Matthew found the dry bones of Ezekiel's vision comparable to the passing of Jesus through death to life (Matt. 27:52–53).

At stake in the classroom is truth, not temporary satisfaction for the students. The truth is uncertain, in the realm of probabilities and problematics. There is ongoing research, and gaping differences of opinions concerning the miracles recounted in the bible. A student may be immediately satisfied with an authoritative answer, with a presentation of selected data which reenforce one viewpoint. But then the student's confusion is merely delayed. Eventually the difficulties will be encountered and a too-tranquil faith may shatter on impact. The real danger seems to come from an accumulation of provisional explanations having been presented as though they were the final insights. How difficult it is for an adolescent crossing the threshold of metaphysical thought to revise so much religious lore—the notion of good and bad spirits fighting each other with swords, the need to prescind from ancient cosmology in understanding the religious testimony of the bible, and then the need to reconcile the notion of God as designer of nature with its consistent "laws" and his inconsistent "exceptions to the laws of nature"!

CONCLUSION

The gospels were written to manifest Jesus. The miracle episodes present Jesus as one who cares and one who cures.

Each person in a sin-tainted world stands in need of care and of rectification. This is the scope of religion. The Good News is not a rival to medicine. Indirectly an incarnated God is sensitive to bodily anguish. But the modern evangelist may well imitate the gospel writers by treating physical miracles casually, while concentrating on the portrait of Jesus. The gospel portrait reveals a man preoccupied with God and anxious to cure his fellow humans of all that alienates us from being more fully brothers and sisters within his family. Marginal items should not be so emphasized that one neglects the person in that portrait.

It is paradoxical but an unfounded clarity in teaching biblical miracles may compromise students' faith in the essential message of scriptures and will likely blur the picture of Jesus presented in the gospels.

7

TEACHING THE
COMMANDMENTS

A third biblical element deserving the religious educator's attention is the place in the syllabus for the commandments. In recent centuries these rules from the Mosaic moral code have assumed a prominence which is not reflected in the scriptures nor in overall tradition of Judaism or of Christianity.

In designing religious syllabi educators must select some items for intense study and must allocate less stress on other items. In such decisions the totality of one's religious and educational acumen is likely to be involved. But other input may be felt too—pressures from concerned parties (parents, pastors, authors of textbooks, exponents of law-and-order, exponents of more liturgy, more doctrine, or more morality), personal nostalgia for prolonging one's own childhood experiences, a hesitancy to "be first to put aside the old" or of being last "to take up the new."

A current example of this ambiguity is offered by the ten commandments. Some modern religious educators bypass or deemphasize the decalogue, with suasive arguments for this policy. Other educators disagree, with cogent reasons for giving much attention to the Mosaic commandments.

Both views can be substantiated with scriptural citations along with reputable interpretations of the texts. The Sinai theophany is presented as a peak experience. For it occasions cosmic phenomena (Exodus 19:16; Deut. 4:11; 5:22), lyrical reflections (2 Kings 18:6; Bar. 2:28; Sir. 45:3), and liturgical commemorations (Pentecost festival). Jesus explained his retention of Old Testament Torah (Matt. 5:17). But Jesus seemed ambiguous about the commandments (Mark 10:19–21 and parallels), or to favor supplanting them (Matt. 22:40). Paul too suggested a Christian attitude displaces commandments (Rom. 13:9–10), but he still esteems tbe commandments (Rom. 7:12). Texts and exegeses seem to leave the role of the decalogue in a Christian educational program problematic.

Critics have indicted the commandments as negative, pre-Christian, as an oversimplification of morality, suited to a primitive, tribal society. These four judgments are certainly true.

REFLECTIONS

But laws are generally negative in wording, for they demand a minimum standard of performance. However the study of Torah has always included study of the lives and examples of those who lived Torah, those on whose hearts are written the law of life (Jer. 31:33). Thus the negative wording of the commandments is offset by the positive wisdom and beauty of those whose lives affirmed the spirit in which these prohibitions were understood—Samuel, David, Daniel, Maccabees, etc.

Both God and mankind are pre-Christian. So morality, the regulation of religious and social obligations, also antedated the Christian era. We must not read pre-Christian as provisory. St. Matthew was cautious about trying to patch together irreconcilable doctrines (Matt. 9:16–17). But he chose to introduce Jesus as Teacher by sketching a moral discourse on a mountain, with Jesus several times introducing topics with the words, "Moses said to you ... but I say to you. . . ." Subtly he suggests a harmony between Jesus the Teacher and the pre-Christian Moses.

The commandments simplify morality; they are a summation. But from their inception they inspired commentaries (Pentateuch, Talmud, etc.), interpretations (priestly code, scribes, rabbis, etc.), and derivatives (Essenes, Sadducees, etc.). If the decalogue is faulted for over-simplification what judgment will be passed on the further simplification suggested by Jesus (Matt. 22:40) and Paul (Gal. 5:14)?

The mores of a tribal culture do seem somehow less sophisticated, less complex, and more limited than the complex customs, regulations, and behavior modification factors at work in a technological nation. But it may be that simplicity is not a fault in an ethical system, nor should we a priori presume complexity is an asset to a culture or to its moral system. Doubtlessly all of us are descendants of (or ascendants from) an ancestral tribal culture. We are of the same species as our remote ancestors. If there are universals in morality we might pinpoint them by seeing what values in antiquity are still normative. If the commandments were venerated in a tribal society and are still conditions for imperial societies and for democracies, they might more rightly be termed transtribal or metatribal. Only a victim of tunnel-vision would scorn such items as loyalty, humor, art, nutrition, and tools because they first characterized tribal societies.

JESUS AND COMMANDMENTS

The apparent ambivalence of Jesus concerning the decalogue may be understood as an urgency to personalize religious actions. Not that Judaism had not suggested the eternal existence of Torah (Sir. 24) at God's throne, and proposed affection for the commandments (Psalm 118, espec. vv. 19, 32, 35, 42). But Jesus gave a new mystery to Torah—legislation seen in words, even words from God, ceded place to the unique Word of God who was to dwell in a renewed covenanted community. *Observance* was to be overshadowed by unconditioned divine *love* and an unconditioned human love on the part of those acting by virtue of the charity infused among his followers. So legalism, ascetical exercises, casuistry were all assimilated to personal affection. As advocates of situational ethics are discovering "love is a many-splendored thing," understood analogous to one's own experiences. So Jesus did not abandon commandments and substitute love. He kept the legislation and gave an interpersonal, positive, open-ended, affective dimension to life under law.

If Jesus telescoped the commandments to two obligations the result is not simplification. Persons are mysteries. Love is never programmed or packaged. Jesus gave a vital, inner, guiding Spirit to prompt Christian decision making. He called his gift the Spirit of Truth. Discernment became a privileged task for the people of the renewed covenant. The great care with which the writings were preserved, copied, and proclaimed now was to be applied to discerning the Spirit's influence. The precision of *iotas* and *tittles* (Matt. 5:18) and the reverent hesitation in pronouncing the Sacred Name were exercises in loving fidelity to the written word. But the fidelity in hearing the Spirit's call to careers, to use of charisms, to major and minor choices became a sacred task for both individuals and institutions in the renewed covenant community. The community gradually discerned its own identity—not merely chosen descendants of chosen patriarchs, but as temples of the Holy Spirit, persons spiritually buried and risen to a life that spans time, space, and divisions between individuals.

CONCLUSIONS

After these reflections practical questions remain. Are the Mosaic commandments an adequate moral code for Christian adults or children? No. Should the commandments then be eliminated from the syllabi? No.

The commandments should be taught, and with respect for their lofty religious insights, their universality, their antiquity, and their potency to produce a community of people with respect for God and for the life and property of fellow humans. But morality was seldom reduced to mere observance of the decalogue—and never without disastrous consequences. Let us quickly summarize three case histories—of two Jews and of one Christian group.

"MORE IS REQUIRED"

Jesus perceived economics and class conflicts were destructive to community. The young man who kept the commandments was told to do something more: to give to the poor and to orient his life to resemble the life of Jesus (Luke 18:18–24). The community Jesus desired would esteem the *anawim*, the distressed class (Matt. 5:1–11), and would eschew the divisions occasioned by external, legalistic preoccupation with impersonal piety (Matt. 23:1–36; John 13:12–17; etc.). In presenting Christian morality the educator's task is to familiarize students with Jesus's words and deeds, with his teachings on the guiding Spirit in his followers, both individually and collectively, and with his subtle teachings on community. Children preparing for the sacrament of reconciliation cannot be sorry for rejection of God unless God is known and esteemed. Children cannot aspire to an amended life unless they grasp the notion of a guiding, helping Spirit within them. Children cannot appreciate the sacramental encounter with an agent of the church unless they are aware of the communal tragedy of evil (Matt. 25:41–45). In other words moral catechesis begins with theology, christology, and ecclesiology. The Mosaic commandments are a helpful tool for one who is falling in love with a forgiving Father, a giving Christ, and a guiding Spirit.

Karl Marx sensed the inadequacy of his own religious education in meeting the problems of the Industrial Revolution. Unfortunately his Judaic background was not profound. He was unable to draw from his religious tradition treasures old and new—jubliee years with the cancelation of long-standing debts, and freeing of slaves, the rights of gleaners to surplus harvests, the leviritic provisions for widows and orphans, tithing, etc. He lost the prophet's confidence that economics was a creature subject to man's prudent stewardship. Marx bowed before economics and urged others to accept the inexorable laws of economics as determinants of human destiny. He concluded that the course of history was fixed; only its speed could be accelerated by fostering revolutions. Marx's courage and carefully prepared work were in the finest tradition of Amos, Isaiah, and Jeremiah. Perhaps they would have applauded Marx's dictum: from each according to his ability, to each according to his need. The idea of a classless society would appeal to John the Baptizer, Jesus, and Paul. For they too worked hard to arouse people to pursue a community wherein generosity was treasured more than acquisitions. In mid-nineteenth century London Marx saw the commandments venerated and observed. But he also saw mounting human misery. He proposed a drastic program to complement the decalogue.

The Baltimore Catechism (a Roman Catholic question-and-answer book introduced by American bishops in the mid-nineteenth century and used almost exclusively in Catholic education for children during the following century) proposed a moral code centered on the commandments. But sadly missing were the complementary elements found in either the Old Testament, New Testament, or in Marxism. On social justice there is silence—unless "corporal works of mercy" are construed as rudiments of a social doctrine. This manual produced for Americans living in the latter half of the nineteenth century never mentioned racism, wars between humans, civil rights, child labor, buying and selling people, intoxication, or genocide. The moral presentation was clear, rooted in Judaeo-Christian tradition, but irrelevant to time and space. The Spirit who spoke through the prophets, who inspired the Evangelists, who makes all things new may have been judged too busy or too awesome to be consulted in Baltimore, or perhaps thought of as too preoccupied with eternal truths to be concerned about here and now problems.

One cannot fault the commandments. They are good, beyond reproach. As with the basic "do good and avoid evil," there is no argument among sane people. But specifics are needed: insights into the implications of the various duties, motives for living according to a code, strategies for dealing with borderline cases in the gray areas, and a sense that the One behind the whole right/wrong realization calls us to come far beyond ethical living to "be perfect as the heavenly Father," to "take up the cross and follow (Mark 8:34)," as the Spirit leads each one (1 Cor. 12:11).

STRATEGY

If parents or pastors fret about neglect of the commandments in children's religious education programs it is well to engage them in patient dialogue. Seldom is their anxiety based on fear that the children are acting contrary to the commandments—eg., by coveting their neighbor's wife or by fashioning strange gods. Often the complaint is that the children's common sense dictates some preverbal code of justice coinciding in practice with the code endorsed by Moses. But they would be delighted if the children could, on request, recite the decalogue, and without groping for words or for ideas. Sometimes lurid stories are told of teenagers who are dumbfounded when asked what is the fourth or the eighth commandment! It may not satisfy the elders but such children are in good company. For Moses (Exodus 20:17; Deut. 5:21), Jesus (Matt. 19:18–19), and Paul (Rom. 13:9) seemed to have trouble with the "right" sequence of the commandments!

How should the commandments be inserted in a catechetical program for children? This is a problem. Research by Piaget, Elkind, Simon, and Kohlberg indicates that children develop a moral sensitivity over a period of years. Modern catechists would certainly hesitate to bypass these findings by presenting to children at the beginning of their moral development a scheme Moses presented to an adult group whose experiences of both evil (Egypt) and good (Exodus) were vivid and recent. The present generation of children is well indoctrinated by current morality plays (crime and cowboy shows). As the child is maturing in his or her grasp of freedom there is hopefully a simultaneous clarification of the child's concept of Jesus, God and church. Friendship, love, community are experienced, even though they are still be-

yond the child's verbalization skills. Fair, kind, sharing
friendly, mean, hurt another's feelings—these experiences
become objects of awareness which a child can verbalize.
These items should be the objects for "examination of con-
science," the cause for approval or regret in reviewing one's
use of freedom. Later will honesty, truthfulness, cheating,
pride, impatience, anger, obedience, respect, polite manners
come within a child's moral horizons. Still later will envy,
sulking, neglect of duties, giving harmful or helpful examples,
generosity, cheerfulness, cooperation derive from accumulation of experience in living with various human groups. Only
when a variety of experiences, a deepening of concepts, and a
genesis of moral insights have taken place is a child ready for
the abstract, comprehensive summary of morality in religious
and social life represented by the decalogue. Not only will the
commandments then serve as a convenient synthesis, but
their study can be the occasion for moving into areas of difficult discernment. A child who has a sense of private property and the experience of chaos when ownership is ambiguous can recognize the wisdom in the prohibition against steal-
ing or of coveting the neighbor's goods. But experientially or
vicariously today's child is aware of the gap between "have"
and "have not" individuals and nations. Conflicting rights
pose the moral dilemma for mature people. The growing child
must not be led to believe Moses presented a tidy package of
rather obvious principles. The mature believer's moral and
ascetical life is usually lived in discerning and choosing the
better courses of action, selecting the more appropriate decisions for *me*, at *this* time, in *these* circumstances. The Holy
Spirit, not only Mosaic dicta, is operative in such efforts.

Moreover, a premature presentation of the commandments
will inevitably demand much pedagogical footwork to steer
clear of difficulties which might be posed by children who are

too inexperienced to assimilate truthful responses to their questions. A child might ask if the prohibition against coveting the neighbor's wife applies only to men. Only after a sense of history and cultural pluralism has been developed can one comprehend that the ancient Semites regarded wives as property of husbands. In later childhood one can accept the legitimacy of stretching the words of the commandments to imply fidelity in marriage for both men and women. Likewise the maturing child can judge that the avoidance of killing is assured by control of anger, by avoidance of fighting and of intentional injuries. These interpretations are not the teacher's misuse of scriptures to maintain classroom decorum. These are reasonable implications for intelligent and experienced readers of the succinct principles. Other commandments are understood authentically only if one understands polytheism, the concept of sacred times, and polygamy (both simultaneous and successive). It seems much wiser to delay teaching the commandments until students can grasp the context of their origin and the context in which they can direct her or him to the promised freedom reserved for God's People.

SUMMARY

Thus there are reasons for including and for bypassing the commandments in a religious education curriculum. In origin and in the history of both Judaism and Christianity the ten Commandments were never the whole nor the summit of religious behavior. Psychological and pedagogical reasons suggest delaying the teaching of commandments until a child has passed through normal development of concepts of right/wrong, has had religious and community experiences to which these duties can be related, and can see the commandments as an epitome of a larger moral system. For abiding by the ten commandments, in isolation from the profoundly spiritual context in which they originated, will characterize a "gentleman" or a "lady," "a good citizen," or a "well-adjusted person." Much more expected from a "pious Jew" or from a "good Christian."

8

TEACHING THE CHURCH

For Christian educators the church is a key ingredient in the curriculum. But it is not so apparent how or when to teach this element. Often students are predisposed to dismiss the church as rather irrelevant to their faith, or they become ill-disposed toward the church consequent to their studying the church.

PROBLEM OF FRAGMENTATION

The three stages of readiness for learning sketched in chapter 2 may seem ill-fitted for teaching about the church. If the church is taught by describing an institution or identifying the source of religious doctrine there is a genuine difficulty in relating church to the stages of learning. But if the church is presented as a community covenated with God, or as the continuance of the incarnation of God's Son, or as the community of saints, or as an historical effort to clarify and utilize the teachings of Jesus then the church can be taught indirectly within the students' three stages of maturation.

In a comprehensive religious education program there is always the danger of the trees obscuring the woods. Both teachers and students tend to isolate discrete elements for immediate attention. Then more elements are added. What is seen at the conclusion—woods or trees?

In a thorough program, Christian educators agree that scripture, social doctrine, liturgy, church history, non-Christian religions, life of Jesus, personal morality, faith, sacraments, charity, concepts of God, of church, religious arts, the Holy Spirit, contemporary problems, and ecumenism merit inclusion. The instructional program is usually extended over many years. At a given moment during this span of time the teacher is convinced that the item being taught is basic and essential. The alert student soon shares this value judgment too.

The danger is that the student is accumulating odd-sized pieces of a jigsaw puzzle, convinced that each piece belongs to the integral picture. But the student does not see how any *one* piece is fitted exactly to *any other* piece. Even on a smaller scale the student may not see that his learning about tetrachs, scribes, land area of Palestine compared to Vermont, and procurator's duties in the Roman Empire fit into God's salvific plan for fourth-graders. When one does fit a few pieces together it becomes easier to find pieces of the same color to attach to the sections beginning to grow into a subunit.

COHESION

This chapter suggests four elements about which the basic Christian message mediated by the example and by the teachings of Jesus can be structured:

> intimate friendship with our divine Father;
>
> service to people by caring for them and by curing their weaknesses;
>
> reliance on the Holy Spirit;

the function of the community in mediating the gospel message.[1]

t does not seem likely that knowledgable persons will ques-
ion the essential roles of these four items. It seems likely that
rticulation with one or more of these three elements will give
 any lesson being taught a desirable stability, relevance, and
eenforcement. The student who perceives a core to the com-
lexity of Christianity is likely to append personal insights,
eflections, and experiences to this core, thus enriching his
nderstanding of Christianity and of his being a Christian.

Clearly this fourfold scheme is christocentric. Certainly it
ives central place to the trinitarian doctrine. Creation, prov-
lence, liturgy, eschatology, and prayer fit tightly around the
rst element. Incarnation, social doctrine, gospel study, sac-
aments, mariology, and hagiography cluster about the sec-
nd element. Vocation, discernment, mission activity, and
rophetic or charismatic roles pertain to the third element.

Presuming that Jesus is the authority on Christian wisdom
nd concluding that the New Testament presents reliable evi-
ence of the insights of Jesus, teachers of religion and students
re likely to turn to the bible for data about these four elements
 the overall curriculum.

Both the committed and the skeptical investigators find
onvincing scriptural evidence that Jesus and his immediate
ssociates did stress the first three elements. Objectively the
les of Father, Son, and Spirit are sketched in scriptures as
rgiving, giving, and guiding. Subjectively the followers of
esus are urged to develop intimate friendship with the

---

1. This fourfold scheme is also urged in the *General Catechetical Direc-
ry* published by the Roman Catholic Congregation for the Clergy in 1971.
atechetics in Context by Berard Marthaler is a commentary on this docu-
ent (Our Sunday Visitor Press, 1972).

Father, to follow Jesus (by faithful meditation on his word and by a loving imitation of his deeds), and to respond to the inspiring Spirit of Christ in decision-making situations.

It has been this teacher's experience that the data are so clear and so attractive that the generality of students readily affirm that pristine Christianity is all about the triune God and about our relationships to God, to his Son Jesus, and to the Spirit. But the serene and often enthusiastic response of students to trinitarian and personalistic religion often collapses when the topic of church is introduced.

CHURCH: A DIFFICULTY

It may seem that here is the one fatal flaw—the student whose education follows this scheme will not see any essential role for the church. In fact, there are many young people today who esteem God, follow Jesus sincerely, and apparently try to live attuned to the Spirit, but at the same time they attach little significance to the church and to church influences.

Rather than giving new grounds for this error the above skeleton provides three firm supports to which an ecclesiology can be firmly attached as the fourth key element. This would be faithful to the catechetical method used by Jesus. For he did not present any analysis of *church* but he stressed needs which only a community can fill, and functions which can take place only within a community. Jesus did not define an institution. Rather he won friends and collaborators for his ongoing task of establishing the kingdom of God.

Why is this fourth element so disturbing? Logically and psychologically both students and teachers look for the church to serve much like a sandal—to allow us to progress securely over rough terrain, to minimize unhealthy environmental abrasions, to give subtle support and constant comfort. But often the church impresses students as "the pebble in the shoe," for which Latin writers used the word *scandalum*. Sincere students will sometimes say the church is, for them, an obstacle to apprehending God, and thus a barrier to their religious fulfillment. They look for a *sandal*; they find a *scandal*.

Here are some probable explanations for this disillusionment. First, institutions (government agencies, schools, family structure, corporations, churches) are currently suspect, if not openly vilified. Secondly, the first three elements are divinely perfect and are eminently enticing, while the fourth element manifests human foibles and failings to an aggravating degree. Thirdly, the gospels are relatively silent about the church, so one might reasonably question if the curriculum distorts the Christian message by elevating the church to the pedagogical level of Father, Son, and Spirit.

To meet the first disturbing factor (the *institutional* church) the teacher might examine the concept of church being taught. If the "political" aspect (hierarchy, jurisdictional areas, juridical offices, primacy, *pompous* pomp, statistics, finances, areas of influence, and grandiose portrayals of missions, schools, chanceries, checks and balances of power, organized charities, and publications) is overstressed the student may react with the depressing dread commonly felt when one is confronted by mammoth creatures. By contrast good current religious education stresses the personal, the human, the community nature of church. People are usually flexible and are responsive to affection, whereas institutions tend to be rigid and cold. Thus we easily despair about corruption in high places, while we ardently hope for the rehabilitation of the lone criminal.[2]

2. Probably at any one moment each of us regards the church primarily as either "thing" or "persons." Perhaps there is a mine of subconscious implication in the fact that as Christianity spread from the Mediterranean area to

To meet the second disturbing factor (perfect Christ and imperfect Christianity) the competent teachers will use current self-images of the church (always in need of reformation,[3] servant,[4] reconciling[5]), and will avoid triumphalism, such as the equation of God's kingdom, the People of God, and Catholicism. The student who ponders prayerfully the gospels will discover the human weakness of Jesus—his real need for companions, for mutual trust, for attention, water, rest, help, and tolerance. It was not easy for everybody to love the methods or the man who is Mary's Son. The church is not meant to be a mutual admiration society or a jungle wherein the weaker beasts are destroyed by the claws of the stronger. The problems of one's fellow Christians can be the occasion for prayer, compassion, and assistance. One's own misuse of freedom can occasion contrition, humility, and a fresh start in the right direction. Those expecting a flawless church might ponder this suggestion: "If you can find a church that is perfect, by all means join it; but realize that when you do, it has ceased to be perfect."[6]

To meet the third disturbing factor, the paucity of scriptural data about the church (especially in the gospels), one should be honest, recognizing that the gospels do not depict Jesus as concerned about the organization, the future, nor the totality

---

northern Europe the word for the Christian group (*ecclesia* in Latin and *ekklesia* in Greek, *église* in French, *chiesa* in Italian, *iglesia* in Spanish) mean an assembly of concerned people, but the new word (*kirk* in Scotland, *church* in England, and *Kirche* in Germany) meant a building. As Christians we might well analyze our word-associations and our dream representations of the archetypal *church* as it was apprehended in our collective infancy.

3. Vatican Council II's "Decree on Ecumenism," #5.

4. Vatican Council II's "Dogmatic Constitution on the Church," #8.

5. Pope Paul VI in General Audiences on 5/9/73, 6/27/73, 10/31/73. Cf also 1971 Synod of Bishops.

6. *The Great Mysteries*, Andrew M. Greeley (Seabury, 1976), p. 94.

of functions performed by the developed church. Pedantic exegesis of Matt. 16:16ff. never convinces anybody that the church is a central topic in the gospels. The scriptural data for the first three of the four elements are much different from the data about the church. It may be reasonable and honest to call the church an epiphenomenon. Persons who develop intimate friendship with their divine Father, who meditate on and emulate the words and deeds of their brother Jesus, and who are sensitive to the guidance of his Spirit have so much in common that they will have a distinct value-system, an observable lifestyle. They will be gregarious (John 10:16, passim), a subculture (John 13:35), fraternal (Matt. 5:45). The fourth element is a consequent, not a complement, to the first three elements. The church developed a *posteriori* to devout Trinitarian faith. The church should not be presented a *priori* to divine faith and devotion, nor parallel to belief in and love for God. Students are likely to integrate the church between their religious horizons if they study the physiology rather than the anatomy of the church. One might conceive an integral Christianity without attention to the church; given expectations of an immediate *parousia* Jesus and the apostles may have been in this group. There is no great religious mystique in church structure; many of the organizational details are religiously indifferent if not irrelevant. But what those who surrender to Jesus do communally and their esteem for each other's faith and allied charisms are quite important to a follower of Christ. The fact that Jesus came at "the fullness of time," and not at the endpoint of history gives prominence to the age of the church. Thus the functions of the church are inevitable; they derive from the human component and from the historical dimension in which the followers of Jesus now exist. Rather than confronting the student with the towering edifice of church with all its ramifications, jargon, and lyrical narcissism, a teacher need only permit the student grounded in personal dependence, emulation, and receptivity to the Trinity gradually to discover like-minded people. Their interaction will spell church in a dynamic fashion. The student will treasure the church because its members enrich his life and the life of other Christians.

SIX CHURCH FUNCTIONS

What are these unique functions of the church which make her worthy of attention similar to that given to the divine persons in this educational scheme?

First, given the inconsistency of human nature under stress *group support* is needed to assure tenacity on the part of individuals. Cheering sections, bands, pep rallies, school songs can help a weary team to victory. An enthusiastic, prayerful, en-couraging community can aid a wavering believer to "take up his cross and follow." The collective spirit of like-minded people supports the strenuous effort needed to live a lifetime in imitation of Jesus. This is church in action.

Second, the church functions *informationally*. Jesus is not coming to teach each individual of every generation. Some agency must keep alive his teachings, by passing on the tradition and/or by compiling written records. Tradition means the exchange of insights from meditating on the Good News allows me to enrich myself with the achievements of others within the community. For any community has a network of communications (documents, homilies, art works, customs, etc.) to insure that an individual's assets are not limited to his or her own immediate use. The extension of the community through generations of members and through all races, cultures, and classes means that God's very subtle revelation does not have to be repeated by him for each of us. There is a public or catholic proclamation wherein God spoke and speaks to his people collectively. For Christians have consistently sensed that the community as such is moved by the Holy Spirit. Occasionally this realization is obfuscated by such jargon as councils, time-honored customs, credal statements, pastoral letters, and infallibility. But in each of these terms we imply that the group is kept oriented in the right direction by a divine principle whom Jesus called the Spirit of Truth. Some public relations unit must call attention to Jesus and must promulgate his message. This is church in action.

Third, the church *provides models* for Christian living. Usually little attention is given to the church's function in designating saints. But Christianity would be merely a romantic ideology unless it produced and designated real saints. Saints show that Christian holiness is possible—for them and presumably for us too. The array of saints demonstrates how Christian holiness appears in various circumstances. Every group struggling toward a goal benefits from heroes and heroines within its membership. Their strategies are guidelines for others who face confusion in relating the gospel portrait of Jesus to the ambiguities of other careers, with different obstacles, and in dissimilar environments.

Fourth, *crisis intervention* is the role of the sacramental system in the lives of community members. At peak moments, special help from Christ aids one to be born in faith, to assume a mature, public Christian stance, to grow in charity, to overcome alienations, to fulfill key ministries, to form a new family-community and to respond to illness consistent with the Christian ideals. Thus the sacraments are primary aids—not quaint rituals, but apt instruments for meeting the crises which beset earthly life. They are peak experiences wherein life is oriented in rather definitive directions (births, adolescence, career choices, etc.). At these sublime

moments Christ is present to help his followers. This is the
sacramental system. Sometimes people have low esteem for
this sacramental assistance. Having learned to walk, not yet
having felt the slowness from arthritis, we may insist that we
need no "crutch." This sense of spiritual well-being is a
healthy sign. But health maintenance requires use of appropriate preventive means. Proper activities will enhance well-
being. The adolescent who insists no crutch is needed will
often feel no reluctance in using a bicycle or a car to reach
destinations unlikely to be reached by sheer intrinsic effort. It
is to be noted that the sacramental signs do not resemble a
crutch; they do resemble bathing, eating, drinking,
massaging—activities about which normal people feel no
humiliation nor contempt. Sacraments are church activities.

Fifth, the church *correlates* individual efforts. The "turned
on" believer senses the scope of Christ's program. He or she
catches the vision of a world turned around to face truth and
love radiating from God. The practice of "the good life"
sketched by Jesus becomes most important. But soon one
meets societal problems: political, social, economic situations
so pervasive that isolated individual effort at change seems
useless. Here the influence of Christ on the wisdom,
strategies, and team-effort of his followers is found to be effective in situations where the well-intending individual is impo-
tent. The lonely, frustrated, quixotic Christian is likely to find
the thrill of success when he associates his quest with that of
his neighbors. God chose to involve others in his management
of the world. God made humans to be social animals with
organs of communication. God has made moments of communion to be delightful. God made his friends into a community.
In time the student will likely find the church's essence by
first finding the vital functions served by the church in his or

her sustained relationship to Christ. So it follows that church social doctrine is not so much an ecclesial fact as a psychological necessity for believers. Christians conspiring for improvements are the church in action.

Sixth, *celebrating* our living after the pattern of Christ is church liturgy. A party, a dance, a drama, a game all require a number of people inclined to highlight what otherwise could have been a prosaic event. In liturgy, or corporate worship, we give to God the events of our living (work, praying, play, pain) along with Jesus who presents his total life to God. So liturgy should not be taught as if it were an interruption of nonreligious concerns to give or to get anything from heaven within the liturgical ceremony. For in liturgy what goes on throughout the day, all through the week is united in symbol and in reality to the service Jesus offered to God and to God's People. Thus life becomes a gift to God, a gift enhanced by its association with Jesus's earthly but eternal gift to God. The divine response to the human self-surrender of Jesus is extended to the members of Christ's community, so they can live every hour of each day influenced by Christ. All the arts can stimulate all the senses to participate in these symbolic rites. Ritual, whether it is graduation, wedding, military review, funeral, or presidential inauguration, provides a stylized format for what might otherwise be awkward effort to give expression to intense feelings. In celebrating, individuals temporarily lose their self-consciousness by imbibing the spirit of the group. The excited fan does not feel silly in following the cheerleaders' shouting. He does not hear himself, but only the collective cheering of the group. The community absorbs the individual, and the individual rejoices to be freely a part of the community. In teaching liturgy, both scriptures and sacrament (especially the Lord's Supper) are taught in their communal dimension, not merely as book and magic, but as reasons for a group to celebrate God's providing for their heads and hearts to be drawn to him.

In conclusion, it is suggested that teachers present the threefold core elements, that each lesson be developed as a ramification of one or more of the three key elements which Jesus revealed by word and work. Hopefully the students will begin to attach each new part to the familiar framework. Slowly the students will repeat history by discovering the functions which make the church become the fourth key element. For those who heard his word and kept it found themselves united into a tightly-knit group. This mode of teaching as Jesus did has psychological, sociological, and pastoral promise as an instructional method for presenting the four elements. In place of confronting the students with the church and then trying to establish the rationale for the church's existence and activites it is here suggested that the student who looks at the Trinity and at himself will see a part of humanity, potentially all of humanity, in a different light, in an illumination of trinitarian faith. At that moment church will have been learned experientially, subjectively, affectively. The desired outcome will be a cordial introduction of the students by Jesus to each of the divine persons. On reflection one will cherish the church that has and continues to make the Good News known, to make good actions honored, and good lives multiplied.

9

TEACHING THE SACRAMENTS

The previous chapter stressed the desirability of educators concentrating on the church's functions, rather than on analyzing church organization and on judgments about God's esteem for an ideal church. Student impatience with esoteric aspects of the church is a barrier the educator faces. The sacraments often are such barriers. But they can be taught collectively and individually as functions of and for the community. They have survived and evolved because they fill needs of the persons who are church, not because the institutional church is stubborn in clinging tenaciously to arcane wizardry.

Here the author's Catholic background and experience will be very obvious. But the problem of sacraments is by no means only a Catholic problem. Sacred symbols and rites are part of every religion and are a challenge to educators in any religious tradition. Hopefully some of the ideas in this chapter will strike a resonant chord in the mind of each reader.

SECULAR SACRAMENTS

Sacraments are difficult to teach. Maybe the difficulty is artificial. Maybe it comes from trying to teach something which seems unlike any other knowledge the student has attained. Ironically the student has been doing sacraments, communicating sacramentally before s/he had learned to talk.

Sacraments (or any other topics) are better understood if they are seen as elements within a broader category, rather than as *sui generis*, as dissimilar to all other experiences. The "seven sacraments" emphasized by Scholastic writers and by subsequent church councils are Christian sacraments par excellence. Strong feelings, sublime truths, peak experiences are usually recounted by use of symbols. Usually verbal and nonverbal symbols are used simultaneously, to try to ex-press more of the content than just words or just gestures or just pictures would signify. A baby's primitive reactions are very clear, very meaningful—smiling, hugging, crying, trembling. These four universal sacraments are used throughout life to manifest happiness, love, pain, and fear. Nuanced versions of each are developed by individuals and by cultural groups. Applause, kissing, sighing, and screaming are subsequent signs of these same feelings.

Although literacy enriches powers of communication, there is an impoverishment if words alone are used to manifest attitudes and actions. Writers have evolved devices to add to the impact of words: figures of speech, italics, underlining, headlining, boldface type, colors and graphics can give added vitality to the impact that two-dimensional material has on readers. Christianity has consistently resisted *bibliolatry*, the exaggerated emphasis on the written word of God as God's influence on his people. Word and sign, scripture and sacrament, give balance to Christian worship. Without the biblical context worship tends toward superstition; without nonverbal signs worship is prone to abstraction and intellectualization.

The value of sacrament, of action complementing word, is realized in crises. There is an awkward futility in telling a mourner at a funeral, "I feel sorry; I hope you discover unsuspected strength and endurance." But a gift (food, flowers, picture card, etc.) and one's physical presence convincingly tell of care, compassion, response, willingness to make effort to relieve pain. Jesus did not expect scriptures to bear his entire solace and strength to Christians in crises. The sacraments are crisis-intervention, actions whereby Christ comes with unique help in meeting key events in our lives.

TEACHING

The precise number of seven sacraments should not be stressed. For over a thousand years devout Christians did not seem concerned about the exact number of sacraments. Today we count seven, but orders can be considered three similar sacraments for deacons, priests, and bishops. Confirmation can properly be regarded as the completion of the sacrament of baptism; they were not enumerated as two distinct sacraments, but only as two parts of the sacrament of initiation in the early church. At various times anointing the infirm has been interpreted as an aid to recuperation of health and as a preparation for dying. If the effect, the intention of the one administering the sacrament, and the desire of the recipient of the sacrament are sometimes concerned with dying and sometimes concerned with recovery it seems there are possibly two sacraments involved in anointings.

It is important that the sacraments be not presented as mere whimsical actions, arbitrarily done at convenient times in the human life span. They are means of communication, designed for clarity and emphasis (not for obscurity), and are designed to meet urgent needs.

Baptism is for spiritual birth. The gifts of faith, hope, and love assist believers through the trauma of adjustment to life in a Christian atmosphere. Faith gives identity, stability, knowledge, orientation. Hope provides anticipation, endurance, and courage to struggle in an atmosphere not wholly Christian. Charity is to convince the new Christian of his acceptance, of his being cared for, and of his being able to love with more than merely human affection. Water is a symbol for dissolving away whatever is inconsistent with Christ's presence and assistance. Water is an archetypal symbol for birth to life, being a requisite for survival. The minister dramatizes the divine plan whereby we are entrusted to our fellow humans for the derivation and the nurturing of our physical and spiritual life. The gospels consistently use the word *baptizein* (submersion, inundation) for this rite. St. Paul compared this immersion experience to the death-burial-rising of Jesus.

Confirmation is the strengthening of nascent faith, hope, and love. The reenforced believer now not only possesses faith passively, but is empowered to be a witness, apostle, evangelist—one who transmits Christianity as God's agent. Like the Apostles at Pentecost the confirmed Christian has been called to surpass egotism and fear so that s/he becomes altruistic. The confirmed person's anxiety is not to preserve faith, but to share it. Facility in communications was the was the most astonishing event at Pentecost. The pristine confirming made disciples into apostles. The Spirit of the risen Christ comes to give a spiritual priority to the believer who is constantly drawn toward the material, temporal, and finite, with the possibility of creatures obscuring the creative, redeeming, sanctifying persons of God.

Holy Eucharist is understood by Catholics today very much according to the mind of Thomas Aquinas, the great thirteenth-century theologian. He regarded this sacrament as the center of the entire sacramental system. All the other sacraments were seen as related to the eucharist. Thomas pointed out that the church itself consists of the same body of Christ in a different mode of existence. The skilled educator does well to retain Thomistic insights: the eucharist is related to all the other sacraments; there is a mystery about the eucharist (which is the mystery of Christ) which makes every doctrine have a eucharistic dimension. The effective educator will use twentieth-century concepts to illustrate the mystery of Christ as sacramental food and drink. The ecclesial dimension of eucharistic theology has expanded to a social dimension, because the church is no longer seen as a sharply circumscribed body rapidly absorbing whatever is not evil outside its walls. The eucharistic polemics which raged from the thirteenth century through the sixteenth century, from Aristotlelian categories to Nominalism and Cartesian concepts have subsided. Contemporary believers seek unity amid diversity; they do not expect *any* philosophical school to provide adequate terms or ideas for enclosing or divulging the mystery of the eucharist.

To prevent the eucharist from being an adjunct to the Christian faith it is important to stress three moorings which situate the eucharist in the mainstream of our faith: the biblical base, the liturgical base, and the community base.

The Old Testament presents providence thematically in terms of Exodus/Passover. The Word made flesh is God's supreme providence for what would otherwise be sheep without a shepherd. The New Testament portrait of Jesus as one who cares and cures all dimensions of human shortcomings can give the reader sensitivity to Jesus as one nurturing hungry people. The loaves and fishes are in continuity with the narration of the institution of the eucharist in terms of a Passover supper and in the drama of the death/resurrection of the renewed covenant's paschal lamb. The Acts of the Apostles tells of the church's eucharistic life; St. Paul, especially in 1 Cor. 11–14, develops eucharistic theology with pastoral guidelines.

In learning of the eucharist the student should be attentive to the milieu in which s/he meets the eucharistic Christ. In the assembly of the worshiping community, in the place entered at baptism, in conjunction with the liturgy of the Word, in the context of celebrating (with food, liquid refreshments, music) the once-separated-now-united body and blood intimately associate Christ and Christians. Time, space, individuality are dissolved by the power that brought life from death, victory from defeat, enrichment from sacrifice, and freedom from surrender.

In a genuine celebration one's attention is not inward. Self-consciousness is lost in the sense of being a part of like-minded people. When the whole cheering section yells, "Sis, boom, bah; rah, rah, rah!" nobody in the group feels silly. Feelings are shared. The individual's self-awareness is dissolved into the group's experience. Holy Communion is such a communal experience. The goal is not personal peace (if such an entity exists), nor joy, nor oneness produced solely by the coming of Jesus. The goal is to care for other people as Jesus does. The eucharist should not be presented as "part of the Mass," but as a way to live each hour of every day—as a Christian among Christians and potential Christians. Justice, social doctrine, sexuality-marriage-family life should be eucharistic. For Jesus is the source of right-living in all aspects, and is the center for discovering love which unites all divisive human predicaments. The challenge to faith is not merely to believe that Jesus is present eucharistically, but to be convinced that we can love with more than human affectivity, and that the other communicants have a new dignity and ability to cherish me in a helpful way.

The challenge to believe in unique Christian charity is specified in the sacraments of vocation: *holy orders* and *matrimony*. For these vocations bring extremes of consolations and of frustrations. The deacon, priest, and bishop encounter people at their best and worst, in their happiest moments and in their saddest hours. In all these services the clergyman is expected to portray Christ, to care and to cure. He is the church's agent and spokesman. He brings Christ's words, sacraments, and loving care to bear on the human situation, especially "to the least of my brothers." Holy orders is a convenient topic for a "loose" rather than rigid insight into sacraments. The extent of trust which Jesus gave to his church is apparent when we reflect that sometime after the earthly life of Jesus the deacons were introduced (Acts 6), that the ceremony of ordination has had changing elements (prayer formulas and actions), that the distinction between priest and bishop and layperson has only gradually evolved, that women deaconesses and abbesses were once prominent in church functions.

Probably marriage as a sacrament is appreciated only after family love and sexual love have been discussed on both the natural and the spiritual levels. Christian marriage is a specification of functions within the eucharistic community. Each family is to be *one* in heart and mind, *holy* in aspiration and in reality, *catholic*, ie., similar in essentials but mixed in manifestations, and *apostolic*, ie., fertile in transmitting a living tradition which shows the life lived by Christ and by his faithful followers. The family is prior to the church both historically and experientially. A Catholic is likely to grasp the true notion of church with the community spirit, tolerance, and service-orientation if s/he has grown in a family which is supportive, respectful, and unselfish.

The *sacrament of the sick* is not an intriguing topic to those who have not had close contact with severe illness. But it can be a subtle reminder that time will bring, sooner or later, a decline in mental and physical well-being. Mortality is reality. Rust and moths can ravage what today seems so beautiful and promising. Jesus has prepared a mansion for us—in his Father's house. But the temporary or lasting decline in vigor need not be accepted with stoic fatalism nor with merely human endurance. Jesus has gone through the door of death. Eucharistically the risen Christ is present among us, to affirm a newer and better life lies on the other side of that mysterious doorway. In the crisis of illness the risen Lord comes with a medicinal sacrament. He cares and he cures. The crisis of sickness and of death are crises of trust. Can we relax our grip on the familiar, on the earthly and the healthy life, to grasp the hand of Jesus who will lead us through the door into our eternal home? A bitter, clenched fist cannot be embraced by the hands of Christ. Life was traumatically poured on us or over us at baptism. That life was nurtured when we opened our mouths for Holy Communion. In the decline of our life Jesus wants us to trust God and to die as he did, without bitterness, without fear in meeting our heavenly Father, the source of all the life and of all the joy we have known. It seems unlikely that on the first Good Friday Jesus regarded his earthly life as completed, with all goals attained and with no loose ends. Nobody meets death with a totally ready attitude. Each of us is challenged to trust the risen eucharistic Christ will gather up the loose ends, will see that we do not leave our friends and our work as orphaned projects. The influence of the saints on people who have not yet passed through the door of death is one part of our faith in the communion (community) of saints. But saintly people, beset on earth by neuroses and diseases, can still be powerful elements in the community if their distress is born in the spirit of Christ carrying his cross. Jesus was prepared for the wooden cross by bearing criticism, rejection, and misunderstandings throughout his adult life. But at these moments of anguish (temptations in the desert, beginning of his public life, agony in the garden) there were messages (angels) and words (voices) of comfort to console him. "In all things I do the will of my Father" is the happiest realization a person can experience. Sickness, depression, ageing are felt as embittering terrors or as parts of God's plans. There is a sacrament to help us live and die with trust and without bitterness, to be Christians rather than to pretend we are earthbound until we are wrenched unwillingly from a life of brevity and ambiguity to a mysterious reality where there is no more dying and where Jesus who gave us life-engendering water at baptism now wipes away the final tears.

Reconciliation is perhaps the most difficult sacrament to teach. For many details are now in a state of transition—the name, the externals, and the emphases are being revised. Undoubtedly pastoral practices will react to these innovations.

As with the other sacraments the teacher of the sacrament of reconciliation should sketch a human phenomenon to which the church brings Christ's special help. People have some freedom. Free actions make us feel either satisfied or guilty. We term them either good or evil. Morality is a problem both for victims and perpetrators of harmful actions. *Metanoia* or reversal is the crucial change of attitude for the sinner. It implies an attempt to rectify, to do what can be done to stop or to undo effects harmful to others or to one's self. Any moral person recognizes the urgency for reversing a destructive attitude. But the rectification effort is often less easily recognized. On occasion when the victim is known and the victim's pain is certain there is a clearly-felt need to apologize, to meet with the victim and to pledge friendship, rather than hostility, in subsequent relations. Seldom will one think "God knows," and so feel no urgency to seek the victim who does not know of the remorse for malevolent behavior.

This sacrament makes sense to the extent that one's faith convinces him that the risen Christ vivifies the faith-community. Sin harms the life of the church, just as holiness gives added vitality to the community. God has not chosen to reveal, to sanctify, to deal with us only as individuals, but also as parts of a community. In the light of this belief one recognizes the need to confront the community, to declare both sorrow and future altruistic intentions. It is not practical to go to the entire church and make apology. So one acknowledges guilt, repentence, and prayerful intentions for future conduct to the agent of the community—to the priest. The priest, on behalf of the community, accepts the apology and encourages the good intentions. This overt response from the community's spokesman is very efficacious as the sinner definitively closes a dark chapter of life and commences a new, brighter chapter without lingering shadows of guilt and powerlessness intruding on future aspirations.

The outcome of this sacrament is reconciliation. This means uniting two separated elements which are meant to be united. The reconciliation exists on three levels: the Christian's life becomes whole, rather than torn by sin's disorienting us from God; the relationship between sinner and God is reconciled by love replacing disregard; the community welcomes back one whose conduct was selfish rather than considerate.

As patterns develop reconciliation will be accomodated to pastoral needs. It may be that this sacrament will be celebrated in two or three ways—on relatively infrequent occasions one will make an appointment to review and preview one's moral life. There will be scriptural readings, praying by penitent and priest together, careful analysis of behavior patterns, and skilled encouragement given by the priest. More often the daily failings will receive sacramental reconciliation in a communal penance service. The scriptures, praying, and

program for rehabilitation will be generic rather than indi-
vidualized. In teaching reconciliation due attention should be
given to the "penitential rite" at the beginning of Mass—a
loose confession of failings, a prayer for forgiveness and
strength, and an absolution formula by the priest.

Since sacraments are usually first taught to children a note
of caution is made here, and with great stress. In relating this
sacrament to the eucharist, avoid confusing sin/guilt/
confession/reconciliation with the specific sacramental effects
of the eucharist. The eucharist should be presented as the
culmination of Christian initiation. In another teaching unit
reconciliation should be presented as the therapy for post-
baptismal sin. Never should the two sacraments be presented
as parts of a unit, nor should they be taught simultaneously.
For all of us finite persons *under*estimate God's love, and we
probably *over*estimate God's vengeance. Generations have
been introduced to the Lord's Supper within the context of
sin and guilt. Their eucharistic lives have been burdened by a
sense of anxiety and a sense of estrangement from Christ. It is
much like administering medicine in the course of a banquet.
To the extent that a communicant's spirituality is sin-centered
it is self-centered and thus it is not christocentric. When reconciliation and eucharist are entangled always does the
eucharist become displaced from its central role, always does
the penitent obscure Christ, always does sin predominate
over love in the total experience of a child, and this inbalance
becomes a lifelong hindrance to healthy Christian living.

CHILDREN AND SACRAMENTS

There are two aspects of teaching sacraments which draw
our attention: the preparation given to children before they
receive the eucharist, reconciliation, and confirmation, and

then the so-called parents' programs often presented at the time the children are being prepared for these sacraments.

In reality a sacrament is a celebration of something prior to and independent of the sacrament. There is, then, a context for a sacrament—a continuity with a nonsacramental experience. To the extent that a child relates warmly to his religious community and to his friend Jesus he will celebrate the eucharist in an informed, beneficial manner. The child who understands obligations, failings, and forgiveness certainly will esteem the gift of reconciliation and its sacramental celebration. The individual who looks closely and critically at Christ and the Christian community and then decides to work within the community for the goals Christ asked his followers to pursue is ready to celebrate the confirmation given him by the Spirit of the risen Christ. In other words sacraments are related to and are understood relevant to the basic components of a religious education curriculum.

To give more intensive educational effort to a presacramental program than to other parts of the syllabus is misleading. Surely sacraments are sacred actions of great significance. But so is the study of scriptures, of Christ, of church, of social doctrine, and of the other essential elements in a religious education curriculum. To build up extreme expectations of sudden, mysterious transformations at the moment a sacrament is celebrated for the first time is likely to buildup for a letdown. Life and growth are gradual, rather than in spurts. Even more deplorable is a program which relies on either anxiety or sentimenatlism to fix a child's attention on a forthcoming sacramental celebration. At these turning points in a Christian's coming of age it does seem very appropriate that the child or youth be interviewed apart from the group, so unique problems or assets can be recognized and appropriate guidance given. Both religion and persons are too important for herding people into an exclusively group-preparation for sacramental life. The sacraments should be the occasion for clarifying one's identity, not for obscuring it by decisions made by proxies, nor for succumbing to a spirituality congenial to somebody else.

Love and reconciliation are I-thou relationships, and much latitude must be left for a person to work out authentic, appropriate, private relationships with Christ and his community. Confirmation preparation, usually during adolescent years, should have special regard for the individual's freedom. The basic question, "Is confirmation for *me, now*?" should not be answered by others. Nor should a youth who concludes "not for me at this time" be subject to criticism nor pressure to conform to the decision of the majority. Confirmation should not be the occasion for regression to other-directed living, but rather the opportunity to make a courageous decision. Too often confirmation is "part of the eighth-grade syllabus," an inexorable and automatic activity, just another sign of puberty. Confirmation is meant to be the occasion for pledging deeper involvement with Christianity. It has become the occasion for "dropping out" of formal religious practices for too many whose freedom was frustrated by well-meaning educators. The freedom is regained by "going through" the confirmation ceremony and then opting out from the consequences. There is, besides, the complex question: is confirmation (like marriage) invalid if fear or force, rather than freedom, was the prevailing motive for being in the sacramental situation.

Often the parents of children in religious education programs are rediscovered and contacted a few weeks before the children are to celebrate a sacrament. Sometimes these programs for parents are termed adult religious education. But too often they are using parents as instruments in the education of the children. Presacramental parental programs can be legitimate and productive. It is an apt learning moment for parents; they are concerned about their children's religious development. The parents deserve more than coaching in asking key questions or in reviewing lessons with their off-spring. They are capable of much more than talking up a sacrament for a few weeks. If the parents can be stirred up to be knowledgable and enthusiastic about their own religious concerns they will inevitably help their children. Bishop James Pike once said: your *god* is what keeps you awake at night and what you talk about at dinner. Parents cannot fool children with an intense pretense of religious concern until the sacrament has been celebrated. Parents with a habitual concern for their own religious progress cannot help but give an example to reenforce their children's religious aspirations. The consumers in parents' programs should be the parents.

Prebaptismal programs for adults anticipating the baptism of an infant child or godchild run into some difficulties when effort is made to present baptism as a transformation of the infant. The educational program seems much more effective if it impresses on the parents or godparents the meaning of their decision to have the child baptized, their pledge to pursue what seems best for the child—not only by baptism, but by example, prayer, and by that vague activity called parenting. The awesome role of being parents and of being Christian parents of a Christian child is cause for celebration if parents perceive baptism as a gift to them, likely to transform them, so that they become the persons and parents God wants for his child and theirs.

10

THE ART OF NONTEACHING

The teacher of religion finds a variety of terrain—rough, steep areas and smooth, easily traversed regions. Inevitably patches of quicksand are discovered. If the teacher is so stubborn as to move only in a straight line an effort will be made to build a bridge across the quicksand and thus secure lands will be connected. But since these dangerous areas are few and small it is much wiser to detour around them. Here are some spots worth marking on the religious education map—areas to be avoided.

ORIGINAL SIN

This topic is a theological labyrinth. Each new exploration proceeds further and sinks deeper into the quagmire. No intrepid adventurer ever emerges into daylight. Many are lured into adjacent caverns: polygenism, analysis of concupiscence, conjectures about impeccability.

A religious education syllabus without original sin is not like a day without sunshine. Any concept of original sin is dubiously present in scriptures, doubtfully in the pristine tradition. The work of discerning theologians in our generation suggests that the Holy Spirit is asking us to review doctrinal and pastoral aspects of infant baptism—the action wherein original sin has been so enmeshed.[1]

Of course, you and I cannot erase a topic which has occasioned much attention off-and-on for sixteen hundred years. The advanced student of theology will have to reckon with original sin as an historical topic. But it is likely he will not find it serviceable in present-day religious education. So the term and the idea(s) it suggests need not be introduced to those learning the rudiments of Christianity. For if cosmic evil is so certain each student will discover this reality. If the world is disordered, this is experienced, is self-evident, and should not be presented as an item of *faith*. If a child or youth (or adult) is not convinced that everybody is tainted and that every institution is a menace let him enjoy his perception while he can.

LIMBO

A teacher is advised not to step into this unsafe ground. Avoiding this quicksand is relatively easy. For limbo is not found in scriptures nor in church documents, the terrain most familiar to the teacher. Why, then, have worthwhile teachers often wandered into this morass? It seems they have been seeking release from discontent. Limbo draws those who are discontent with the mystery of our own ignorance and those who are discontent with the mystery of God's mercy. Theologians are free to escape their professional frustrations, but not by confusing reveries of fiction and their theological data. In days gone by, various teachings were given a "note" to indicate their relative probability or certitude. The exis-

1. The recent Roman Catholic *Instruction for Initiation of Adults* has much to say about baptism, but no mention is made of original sin.

tence of limbo would have merited the note of *sentimentally consoling*, a low note indeed. In fact it is dubiously comforting when one reflects that God did not reveal any notion of limbo, that in reality the doctrine is as well-founded theologically as is Santa's use of reindeer. If the consideration of limbo is a temporary comfort to students lamenting the prevalence of abortion, it also may be the occasion of a faith crisis when the time comes to unlearn this pious placebo.

DIABOLICAL POSSESSION

Ancient Greeks feared the sirens, mythical and malevolent seducers whose sounds lured helmsmen to steer ships into dangerous waters. Student interest in the occult, the satanic, and other distractions from Christian learning can be a powerful lure to move ever so lightly into a bed of quicksand. Good and evil are real. Freedom to choose means virtues and vices exist. So morality is a part of religious education. But the evil of invisible creatures hardly explains my evil; but in my mind it may excuse my responsibility. If "the devil made me do it," see him about repentence, penalties, and rehabilitation.

But don't the gospels teach about real devils who possess real people? I don't know. There are texts which seem to teach this. Or they may illustrate morality in vivid, dramatic fashion. The ancient Hebrews borrowed from the rich Persian lore of angels and devils, the invisible good and bad beings. At first they were represented as mythical animals, like the winged bulls or cherubim whose statues Solomon commissioned for the Jerusalem temple. The Book of Ezekiel (1:5–14) uses a similar illustration. The sphinxes of Egypt depict the ancient Middle East's idea of strange guardians over dead pharaohs. So scriptural texts must be interpreted cautiously and sometimes tentatively. Very likely the desert experiences of Jesus (Matt. 4:1–12) as he was about to begin his ministry were reworked into a vivid dialogue between Jesus and the devil when the account took written form. The words of Jesus and the desert locale suggest that the Evangelists wished to introduce Jesus as a Moses-like leader—Jesus meets three problems parallel to the Mosaic experiences during the Exodus, and he rejects evil by three statements attributed to Moses in the Hebrew scriptures.

Certainly there may be devils or at least a devil. But the bible is a precarious source for concluding that Christian faith involves belief in the existence of demons who use intelligent, convincing tactics to deceive people into malice.

More skepticism should be shown toward medieval tales of possession. Many persons were persecuted for being in league with the devil. Perhaps they were only quaintly different, mildly neurotic, or those who for some personal reason did not follow the crowd in a time of intolerance toward minority groups. Even greater skepticism should be reserved for accounts of recent diabolical possessions. My limited familiarity with these accounts of possessions shows a thread of consistency about them. The alleged possession always seems to have been in an obscure town like East Cupcake, Iowa, was written about by somebody remote from the incidents being described, written a period of years after the events took place, and with a certain gullibility which the writer presumes the readers share. The devil is always sassy in the opening chapters, somehow his spirit is dampened by holy water flung around the room occupied by the possessee, and in the last chapter the devil shows himself as a sore loser to a holy exorcist who also scores some points in clever dialogue with the bad spirit. In the course of the writings it seems the devil usually throws some furniture around the room, an activity not noticed in the ancient nor the medieval accounts of possession. It has been my experience that those fascinated by such stories do get a certain thrill from these adventures of conflict for high stakes, from the certain-but-not-stated triumph of good over evil, from the shocking language (usually suggested by _____ _____ in the text, and according to the reader's verbal ability he dubs in very foul words). I am dismayed by those who do not seem to integrate these tales into a healthy, positive, christocentric spirituality. To give the devil his due does not demand equal time be given God and satan.

RELIGION IN MODERN MUSIC AND FILMS

The topics and courses not to be taught are numerous; new discoveries occur frequently, more frequently by some of us than by others. For instance, a teacher should beware of the siren of relevancy. For this can entice a rather normal teacher to look for and to *find* a deep spiritual content in any of the top rock-and-roll songs. The presumption is that the students will imbibe religion in a painless way if the teacher only points out the latent spirituality to the adolescent whose body is writhing in rhythm as a victim of malnutrition manhandles an oversized guitar while describing his spiritual odyssey in terms of taking a trip. A similar quicksand of futility opens up to a teacher whose mind becomes bewitched by the idea that Scandanavian films are not commercial enterprises, not about crooks and sex at all, but all of them tell of man's search for the infinite. The subtitles, the plot, the pictures, and the impression gathered by the unenlightened are all shallow and erroneous. The director, the producer, and the cast are all impelled to do their things because they are mystics caught up in the search for the transcendent. In religious education seeing such films seldom puts students on the trail of the infinite, but the fringe benefits are usually worthwhile: good photography, sometimes an understanding teacher will bring popcorn, and usually if you must excuse yourself and miss any reel or if you can't see the subtitles you are in no way disadvantaged in your grasp of the message.

RELIGIONS OF THE WORLD

Courses such as World Religions can sink many teachers. There is much to be said in favor of teaching about religion as a universal phenomenon, about finding themes among major religions, about preparing students to move into a world of spiritual pluralism. But here a half loaf is better than a bakery. For conscientious teachers will feel the urge to read up on ancient Arctic religions, inner worship in Outer Mongolia, and prehistorical cults on Atlantis. Such courses often become mere litanies of divinities with quaint names dispersed with a density of about two per square mile over the earth's surface. Or a rich variety of religions are carelessly classified as African religions or Indian religions. In many cases a course on comparative religion does not succeed because the students lack sufficient knowledge of their own religion to make any intelligent comparison. A sincere, believing teacher need not stress the superiority of the "home team" religion. But very often a teacher can aid students to appreciate the doctrine, practices, and art of other faiths. Stressing the bizarre or quaint features of other religions may hold student interest, but its learning value is usually minimal, and it is a strategy we would resent if it were turned on our own religious tradition. If students study other religions so as to respect other believers, to become aware of their religious practices, to sense a spiritual appetite among all human groups, to esteem the various symbols devised to express our highest aspirations the teacher has been quite successful.

GRACE

Grace may seem so central and so clearly understood that it should not be displaced from curricula. But the centrality of grace comes from its elasticity. Grace is a thing; grace is a relationship; grace is a condition; grace is uncreated and created; grace cannot be felt and grace can be known experientially; grace is given unconditionally and grace is lost if conditions so determine; grace is individual and communal; grace is and is not charity, Holy Spirit, virtue; grace is unmerited and is merited; is increased but is not quantified. The descriptive adjectives used with grace add confusion—sanctifying, actual, sacramental, lost, mystical, extraordinary, initial, special, mediated. Often disclaimers are introjected, to affirm that grace is not a thing really, is not quantified, nor measurable. But there remains in the connotation of grace a notion of "thingness," with a "more" or a "less" aspect.

In general, religious educators' task is to present religion to people whose lives have many facets. By minimizing special religious jargon the learners can associate religion with other areas of her or his life. Grace is not a familiar term outside of religious discourse. Its use tends to segregate religious thought from the other areas of human living. Younger learners are apt to be confused by the associations they bring to the word grace. Grace is a female name; grace is a prayer at mealtime; grace refers to executive pardon given to condemned criminals; grace comes from dancing classes.

In keeping with current personalist philosophy one can usually use the term "friendship with God" to replace grace. Then there is less ambiguity, less reification, and much richer overtones. For a person's self-acceptance, actions, moods, and ambitions can be changed by friendship. This last statement is not in the realm of faith. It is the experience of the students.

SACRAMENTAL PROGRAMS FOR PARENTS

Quicksand attracts a teacher whose intention is to entrap disinterested adult students. For about ten years everybody has been saying "adult religious education is the thing." They mean it is the thing for adults next door or across the street, or for those pathetic people "glued to their TV every night." So teachers feel a strong urgency to teach adults. Most adults don't feel the urgency to be educated. The keen-minded teacher soon makes a discovery—many adults are parents and they take this task seriously. So sacramental programs for parents of children about to receive any of the sacraments appear. It's adult religious education. It goes over—with a little nudging like this: "concerned parents are expected to enroll."

Usually such programs tell parents what role they are to play, what image they are to project, what routine they are to follow as their child prepares for holy communion, confirmation, etc. But this approach suggests phoniness. Religion is being used as a tool to do a job. Parents are asked to be pseudoreligious so as to be superparental. Implicit is the opinion that "religion is for kids." The parents are being written off as being too little concerned about God to communicate easily and naturally with their child on spiritual topics. Playing at piety is not enough to be called religious education. To appear suddenly God-centered and to maintain this pose until the sacrament has been celebrated may be difficult achievements, but they prostitute religion.

There are legitimate programs for parents. They consider the parents' personal faith commitment. They do not merely use the parents as indirect religious tools to reach children rather continuously. Here are four elements which can make a sacramental program for parents worthwhile:

how to be more fully Christian;

how to communicate more effectively with children, especially in the area of religion, and on the topic of the upcoming sacramental celebration;

a review of key ideas and developments in sacramental and pastoral theology;

an *honest* affirmation that parents are the primary educators of their children, with trust in the *parents* doing the task well if they are religiously educated adults.

In many places fertility has become a requisite for enrollment in adult religious education programs—family-centered or parent-centered programs. Or at least nubility is required—for marriage enrichment, marriage encounter, Cana Conferences, spirituality for the divorced, etc. These programs are good and are needed. But other programs should meet the needs of the unmarried, the childless, the senior citizen, etc.

OPTIONAL DEVOTIONS

The list can be extended to topics of doubtful universal religious value: some legends about saints which tend to present saints as "weird, zany people," hymns whose translators maintained the proper number of syllables and the rhyme by befuddling the meaning beyond comprehension. Private devotions attractive to a teacher may not appeal to students. Thus your scapular may prove a millstone around my neck; your pious medal might choke off my spiritual breath; your relics may be deadly stimuli to my devotion; your Compline may put me to sleep; the "act of contrition" prayer attributed to St. Augustine or to St. Alphonsus may provoke an identity-crisis if God is expecting to hear from Bob O'Brien of twentieth century U.S.A. Rosaries, reparation to the Sacred Heart and/or Immaculate Heart, candlelit shrines in the living room, grottoes in the backyard, dashboard religious art, delight in the diocesan newspaper, curiosity about Portuguese deadletters, Corita Banners, plaques with such wisdom as "Life is Loving" and fonts of holy water where one expects to find light switches may not be my cup of tea.

The concentration on noncontroversial essentials is reflected in the recent textbook series for children (Sadlier, Benziger, Paulist). Andrew Greeley's recent *The Great Mysteries* (Seabury, 1976) is a fine example of its claim to be an essential cathechism, while it bypasses purgatory, benediction, particular and general judgment speculations, and other favorite indoor sports of religious educators.

CONCLUSION

The purpose of this chapter is to suggest that greater clarity and freshness will come from more selectivity, ie., from a readiness to omit some traditional terms or units which no longer seem to contribute to a balanced curriculum. The author does not subscribe to iconoclasm nor to being impatient with "the faith of our fathers." But somehow that faith must be polished to shine, not left encrusted with confusions coming from expressions more suited to a bygone era.

CONCLUSION

Obviously this book fails to consider all the important issues in religious education. Although organizational structures, budgeting, and administrative procedures merit much attention, they have not been discussed here. Since details differ so much among schools, school systems, released time programs, after-school religion classes, diocesan, parish and interparochial programs specifics can only be considered in the light of the unique local efforts with its own history and orientation. Perhaps there is too great a readiness to attempt to better religious education by a turnover in personnel, by an administrative overhaul, or by pouring more money into lagging programs. If there is clarity about religious education as a commodity delivered to consumers success is most probably forthcoming.[1] The structure, scheduling, personnel, sites, and financing then become items to foster efficiency, but are not expected to determine success or failure of the overall endeavor.

---

1. There is a persisting tendency for efforts to improve religious education to focus on teachers rather than on learners. Harold William Burgess (*An Invitation to Religious Education*, Religious Education Press, 1975) summarizes and evaluates four current and dominant theories about religious education. *Teacher* and *student* are two of the six categories analyzed by Dr. Burgess. In treating these four major theories 28½ pages concern *teachers*; 11½ pages pertain to the *student* category.

Important, interesting, speculative questions have been overlooked in this book: is religious education a discipline or a field? Is religious education, or Christian education, or Catholic (Lutheran, Presbyterian, etc.) education, or formation, or catechesis the most appropriate term for the task under consideration? Centralization and decentralization of religious education programs are perennial problems. Minischools in homes, correspondence courses using books or cassettes, intense weekends vs. diffused scheduling, family-centered programs, public relations in support of religious education programs, alternatives to parochial schools, diocesan/synodal/regional/municipal/parish/ecumenical responsibilities in religious education are topics for careful consideration on other occasions. A practical item, audio-visual aids (materials, equipment, integration), was omitted. But audio-visuals can contribute very much to clarity in learning each of the topics discussed in this book.

Only a fleeting overview of some areas of religious education has been attempted. But the inspection began with the consumer. By beginning here with those who are nurtured by God's influence there is a probability that key administrative and metaphysical questions will be met wisely, daringly, and with a person-centered approach. There is a parallel: what comes out of the pipe into the gas tank should determine much of the petroleum industry's planning for exploration, drilling, refining, and transmission of fuel.[2] So providing opportunities for students to grow in resemblance to Christ is the goal of Christian religious education. The budget, organi-

2. A sometimes lonely, but convincing voice is that of Iris V. Cully. In *The Dynamics of Christian Education*, (Westminster Press, 1958) she asked educators to turn to "the persons to whom the good news is to be addressed" (76). Her student-centered approach is presented consistently in her *Children in the Church* (Westminster Press, 1960).

zational structure, scheduling, materials, and evaluation are means. About means there can be viable alternatives and there can be frequent changes. But the means are measured by their efficiency in advancing persons toward their goal.

While you have been reading this book the ideas it presents have grown somewhat stale. The hopeful note is that you have grown, not stale, but thirsty. New ideas are rushing over the threshold of current discovery. Run to meet them, embrace them, but be ready to release them when the next issues of the journals appear, when new books arrive, and when fresh suggestions are given. It is difficult to stay abreast in religious education.

There is an urgency to implement the best ideas that experience and research are yielding. For the present generation of learners cannot be plowed into a field destined to grow luxuriantly in the next generation. The future is *now* for today's Christian. Society is changing rapidly. The time-gap between the best ideas and the best programs must be shortened. If parishes, schools, etc., are one step behind in implementing the hard data generated by research, they are hopelessly passé. It is the difficult fact that the journey of individuals and of the human race through life is evanescent. The religious educator must thirst to learn, not to recall what was learned.

Religious education shows much promise. For newness is more readily accepted in this area of religion. For gifted, sincere people are working hard, thinking carefully, dialoging, discerning, criticizing, improving details in the area of religious education. So there is a founded presumption of progress extending into the future. The task of continuously integrating new material into a religious educator's vision will be more orderly, selective, and useful if clarity is habitually esteemed and pursued. None of us need wait for printed

pages to indicate the paths to clarity. No author is more familiar with a particular program than its director is; no writer
knows a classroom situation so well as does the teacher in that
classroom. Clarity is an inviting challenge to everyone in religious education.

ACKNOWLEDGMENTS

The Living Light, from the articles "The Church as the Cohesive Element in Religious Education" in the Summer 1975 issue; "Church: Sandal or Scandal?" in the Winter 1975 issue; "Catechesis for Children" in the Spring 1978 issue.

PACE, from the articles "Mount Sinai Revisited—On Curricula and Commandments" in February 1977 issue; "Biblical Miracles: A Problem for Teachers" in December 1976 issue.

Religious Education from "Packaging Religious Myths" in May-June 1975 issue, published by The Religious Education Association, 409 Prospect St., New Haven, CT 06510. Membership subscription available for $20 per year.

Religion Teacher's Journal, from the article "Let's Begin With a Prayer" in April 1976 issue.

INDEX